How to Write First-Class Memos

the handbook for practical memo writing

L. Sue Baugh

Printed on recyclable paper

NTC Publishing Group
Lincolnwood, Illinois USA

CONTENTS

PREFACE

▼

The *Handbook for Memo Writing* is designed to help you find quick, concise answers to many of your memo writing problems.

WHAT DO YOU NEED TO KNOW?

Whether you need to know more about a specific writing problem or about the memo writing process in general, the strategies in this handbook can help you. Each chapter is designed to deal with specific questions about how to create effective memos. You can go directly to the chapter that answers your questions or work through the entire book. The chapters cover the following topics:

1. *Do you really need to write a memo?* Chapter 1 discusses whether the written or spoken word is the better way to communicate your message. Perhaps your best strategy is to talk over the matter rather than to put it in writing. The chapter offers guidelines for judging when to send or not to send a memo. We also show how learning to write clear, concise memos can enhance your career.

2. *What are the most common mistakes memo writers make and how can you avoid them?* In Chapter 2 we provide a checklist of common errors that most writers make in creating their memos. We then suggest ways to avoid these errors and offer a three-step method of memo writing: preparation, writing, review.

3. *How do you start, what should you cover, and how do you* *organize your message?* As shown in Chapter 3, "Preparation," all memo writing boils down to answering four key questions: What is your purpose? Who are your readers? What is the scope of your message? What response do you want?

We provide key writing strategies to help you answer these questions and to overcome writer's block at any point in the preparation stage. The chapter ends with a series of formats for organizing your memo quickly.

4. *How do you turn your rough draft into an effective memo that gets the reader's attention?* Chapter 4, "Writing," reviews memo format and presents key strategies to add energy and power to your writing. You also learn to use tone, vigorous verbs, and brevity to bring your message to life and get the results you want.

5. *How do you make sure your memo is concise and error free?* Chapter 5, "Review," provides a checklist to ensure that you have answered the four key questions, revised your language, and checked your facts. We also present a brief grammar and style review and a systematic method for proofreading your messages.

6. *What are the guidelines for handling memos in the electronic office?* In Chapter 6 we review office automation systems — LANs and electronic mail systems — and offer guidelines for keeping your memo correspondence in good order. Although computer-generated memos are convenient, they can also be a problem if they are not labeled and filed properly.

SPECIAL FEATURES OF THIS HANDBOOK

Whether you are a beginning or an experienced writer, you should find several features of this book particularly helpful.

■ *Writing Strategies*. The writing strategies presented in Chapters 3, 4, and 5 make use of your analytical and spatial abilities. They not only help you to organize and write your message more quickly but also show you how to take advantage of your mind's natural organizing capacity to improve your writing.

■ *Memo Models*. Chapter 7 presents nearly 70 model memos covering the most common business situations: announcements, congratulations, dismissals, instructions, procedures, and so on.

Each model is accompanied by brief guidelines on how to organize and compose the memo.

■ *Grammar and Style Review*. Chapter 5 offers a review of basic grammar and style covering punctuation, subject–verb agreement, abbreviations, capitalization, and numbers. Business writers often have the most difficulty with these grammar and style points.

■ *Frequently Confused and Commonly Misspelled Words*. Appendix A to the handbook lists words that are commonly confused (e.g., *formerly, formally*) and provides clear examples to show correct usage. Appendix B provides the correct spelling for many words commonly misspelled in business writing.

Memo-writing skills can be a great asset to you in your business career. The strategies and examples in this handbook can help you learn how to write concise, effective messages that communicate rather than merely inform.

ACKNOWLEDGMENTS

Several individuals gave generously of their time and expertise during the development of this book. Special thanks go to Mr. Robert Hansen, Manager of Planning at Ameritech Services in Schaumberg, Illinois. He provided valuable information on office automation systems and offered excellent tips on writing and filing memos via electronic media.

Ms. Caroline Newton, a corporate communications consultant, provided many excellent suggestions regarding memo format and organization for the model memos in Chapter 7. Her sage advise improved many of the guidelines for writing various memoranda.

We would also like to thank Encyclopaedia Britannica for permission to use their letterhead.

"SEND ME A MEMO"

▼

Geri caught up with her harried boss in the hallway.

"Mr. Grant, I found the ideal accounting software for our firm. It has . . ."

"That's great, Geri." Her boss stepped into a waiting elevator. "Send me a memo with all the details by Friday. I want to move on this as soon as possible."

"Have you seen the latest memo from Hal on that corporate tax conference he attended?" Bernard asked.

"Oh, that," Phyllis said. "I'm waiting for the memo that *explains* it. Do you have any idea what 'we need to be more savvy taxwise' means?"

Robert gave his assistant a handwritten memo.

"Jean, type this up and send it to everyone on the staff, will you? I need the meeting agendas by Wednesday morning."

"I don't believe this." Lois looked up from her interoffice mail. "Dale in purchasing just sent me a memo asking if I wanted ivory or white marked on my paper supply order. Why didn't he just call me? This guy is memo-happy."

"The London office wants information on that corporate bond devaluation matter right away," Lorraine said.

"We can fax them Sasaki's memo," her boss replied. "There should be a copy on file."

After a key sales meeting, Tomu consoled Helen, who had been against the group's decision to target an older consumer group for the company's clothing line.

"Are you sure it's going to be such a mistake?" Tomu asked.

"Mistake?" Helen said. "It's going to mean one mass of red ink for this company. The sales manager never even looked at the marketing data for this region."

"If you feel that strongly, why not put it in writing? Send your boss a memo outlining why you think the decision is wrong. Maybe she'll make them reconsider it."

As THESE EXAMPLES show, a memo can be one of the most versatile, efficient ways to communicate within an office or among office branches. It can also be one of the most overused and abused of all office communications.

How do you write an effective message that *communicates* rather than merely *informs*? When is it best to use a memo? How can becoming a good memo writer help to advance your career? In this chapter we address these key questions.

THE WRITTEN WORD VERSUS THE SPOKEN WORD

A memo is meant to inform, to persuade, and above all to communicate to satisfy the *reader's needs* and the *writer's purpose*. Unless these goals are met, the memo fails as a method of communication.

Except for simple announcements, you are not merely passing on information in a memo but telling your readers why the information is important to them. In this respect, the written word has several advantages over the spoken word.

■ *You have an opportunity to think through your message.* In conversation, you can't call your words back or stop to reorganize them into a more logical form. Most people tend to speak off the cuff.

■ *The reader can consider your message at leisure.* With the spoken word, the listener has to catch your meaning as you talk. Because people remember only about 25 percent of what they hear, most of your message is lost.

■ *You can supplement your written message with diagrams, charts, illustrations, and other materials.* When speaking, you are limited to a few gestures. Even if you use audiovisual aids while you talk, the listener's attention may be divided between you and the visual aids. Your message can be the casualty.

■ *Written messages can be filed away "for the record."* Unless recorded, spoken messages disappear once they are delivered. Should a dispute about message content arise, it's your word against someone else's. A written message, however, can be filed away for future reference.

USES AND ABUSES OF MEMOS

Given these advantages, is the written word always better? Not necessarily. Writing takes time and thought. Your memo must be delivered and read before you can receive a reply. If the receiver doesn't check his in box or is away from her terminal, it may mean a longer delay before you get an answer. In addition, poorly written memos or an overload of memos can interfere with good communications and cost companies time and money. High-tech electronics can multiply memo errors at the speed of light, making it difficult to correct them.

Before putting your thoughts on paper (or on a computer screen), ask yourself, "Is a memo the best method to communicate what I have to say?" This question will force you to think about the content and purpose of your message and its intended receivers. For example, you need to ask a question about a new pricing schedule for your company's paper products. Is the question involved enough to require a memo, or can you settle the matter with a telephone call to the sales manager?

It can be helpful at this point to think of yourself as being involved in a personal communications network in your company. (The network can be outlined as shown in Exhibit 1−1.)

Exhibit 1−1. Personal Communications Network

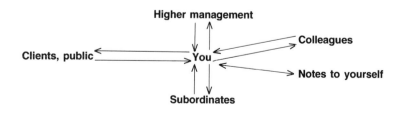

Your role and function within the company will determine your relationship with each group in the network. Do you report to higher management daily, weekly, monthly, semiannually? Do you have frequent contact with clients and/or the public? How often do you communicate with your colleagues and subordinates? Do you write reminders or messages to yourself to help organize your work day?

In your communications network, you can choose to communicate (a) in person; (b) through electronic means (telephone, message recorders, beepers, etc.); or (c) through the written word (memos, reports, letters). Most day-to-day situations can be handled in person or over the telephone. These methods are quicker, permit mutual give and take, and help to build personal relationships with others.

In some situations, such as making an announcement, any one of the three methods will do. The choice is largely a matter of personal preference or style. However, there are messages and situations for which a memo is decidedly the best choice.

When to Send a Memo

In general, the following situations call for a memo as the most effective means of communication:

■ *When you need to reach many people with the same message.* The memo is an ideal form of communication when you need to convey information to a group of people, whether a single committee, a department, or the entire company. Typical messages include changes in company policies or employee benefits; notices of meetings, special outings, and company events; announcements of new hirings, promotions, transfers, and the like; reminders to employees of actions they need to take (forms they need to fill out or return, requests or orders they need to turn in); and general statements on the status of the company (sales records, earnings statements, dividends, etc.). Copies can be distributed easily via interoffice mail or through computer networks.

■ *When you have regular reports to send to the same people.* Perhaps you are responsible for summarizing sales or employee productivity data each week for your boss or the head of your department. Or you may be required to submit bimonthly reports on production. The memo provides a good format for such information. It is terse, to the point, and quickly read. You can send copies to all those who need to stay informed.

■ *When you want to summarize or emphasize information that can be useful to your readers.* You can use this format to summarize the results of research; extract important information from a wealth of data; or point out new ideas or product lines presented at conferences, meetings, and other professional gatherings. You don't have to summarize the entire conference or meeting, but only the information pertinent to your company's needs. Likewise, your personal impressions or opinions of the data or event are important only if they contribute to the main topics.

For example, one manager attended a conference on corporate investment in overseas real estate. It turned out that only one seminar out of fifteen was relevant to her company's situation. Rather than summarize all sixteen seminars, she outlined the real estate valuation approach presented in the one useful seminar and recommended its adoption. The memo circulated among top management, and the method was eventually accepted. It saved the corporation considerable time and money in evaluating real estate investment opportunities.

■ *When you wish to send personal messages to individuals or groups.* Such messages include congratulations, acknowledgment of good work, condolences, announcements of personal interest (weddings, births, illnesses, accidents), and encouragement. Memos commending employees can be copied and included in their personnel files.

■ *When you want to stimulate thinking or action in individuals or groups.* Middle and top management executives often send such memos to their staff or department to jog their creativity and initiative. Because the message is in writing, the recipients can mull over the comments or tack the message up in a prominent place where it can be seen every day.

In one instance, the design director of a cleaning products company sent the picture of a mangled detergent box top to his package design group. His memo accompanying the picture noted that the easy-open top was anything but easy. "Can't we do better than this?" he asked. The group went to work, and the result was an innovative snap top that not only opened easily but snapped shut to prevent spills.

■ *When the timing or political climate is right.* A well-timed memo can be used to motivate employees to greater efforts, point out opportunities, sound a cautionary note about a course of action, or head off a problem before it becomes a crisis. Such memos are part of maintaining good communications with management and staff.

If you detect a pattern of employee tardiness in a department, for example, a memo to the supervisor pointing out the problem and asking for solutions may be in order. Or you may detect a potential cash-flow shortage within six months or notice that overdue receipts are reaching too high a level. A memo at the right time to the right person can mean the difference between dealing with a problem now or having to solve a crisis later.

Likewise, the political climate may require that you write a memo "for the record" or that you "copy" notice of an action or opinion to management. Political jockeying and infighting among company personnel is a fact of business life in most firms. You may find yourself in opposition to others on various issues or actions, or you may have to make important, even unpopular, decisions solely on the basis of your own judgment. You may need to state your views, explain your actions, or summarize the proceedings of a meeting in writing to protect yourself politically in the company.

Have a copy of the memo placed on file and/or distributed to all concerned parties. If, in the future, anyone questions your position on the issue, you have a written record of your stand.

These are all sound reasons for sending a memo. However, there are times when your answer to the question, "Is a memo the best means of communication?" should be "no." You will need to convey the message verbally or, in some instances, do nothing at all.

When Not to Send a Memo

Although individual circumstances will vary, the following criteria are good guidelines for judging when not to send a memo:

■ *When person-to-person communication serves your purposes better.* You may need to know someone's immediate reaction to your message. Or you may need to talk over a subject with someone before putting your thoughts in writing. Perhaps you don't fully understand a concept or problem under consideration and you require more information. The written word cannot substitute for the give and take of conversation, nor can it convey the nuances of someone's tone of voice or facial expression.

■ *When you have nothing pertinent to say.* This may seem like an obvious point but often isn't. Top management may ask you and other managers for ideas about new products or marketing campaigns. Even if nothing occurs to you immediately, you may feel compelled to dictate a memo anyway. Unfortunately, it serves as a transparent disguise for the fact you have nothing to say.

It's much better to send along a brief note indicating that you are giving the matter some thought. When an idea strikes, you can write a memo that says something.

■ *When your emotions are running too high.* If you've been passed over for promotion, just had a fiery argument with the vice president of finance, or had a project canceled with little warning—it is not the time to write a memo on the subject. Firing off a broadside can give you an immediate sense of satisfaction, but it can cost you dearly in terms of others' goodwill and respect. You never know whose goodwill you may need in the future.

Give yourself time to cool down, talk the matter over with someone, or find some other way to let off steam. Once your emotions have stabilized, you can write a better message. You may even find that you don't need to write a memo at all but may take a different course of action.

■ *When you have more important duties.* Keep your priorities straight. Don't take time to write a low-priority memo while a client who wants to know what happened to her order waits for your return call. It may be easier to deal with interoffice communications than with an angry client, but first things should come first.

■ *When broad-based criticism is unwarranted.* Some managers fall into the trap of using the "shotgun approach" in memo writing. One manager noticed that three of his twenty salespeople were using the company cars to take care of personal business on the job. Instead of speaking to these people individually, he issued a general memorandum warning all the salespeople not to abuse their privileges and stating that such misconduct could be considered grounds for dismissal.

The innocent salespeople were offended by the memo, while the guilty assumed everyone was misusing his/her company car and saw no reason to change their behavior. The manager aggravated the problem instead of resolving it.

■ *When the timing or the political climate is wrong.* There are times when a decision *not* to act can be a master stroke on your part. In a management consultant firm, for example, the word-processing supervisor instituted a new queuing system to get work in and out of the pool faster. For the first week, the transition from the old system to the new created considerable chaos.

One consultant whose work was delayed found himself sorely tempted to fire off a memo criticizing the new system. He wisely decided to wait a little longer and give the system a chance. By the second week, the word-processing pool was operating smoothly, and his work *was* getting in and out of the pool faster. Had he followed his original impulse, he would have created needless ill will between himself and the word-processing supervisor.

In the same manner, office politics may dictate when to refrain from writing a memo. If someone requests your views in writing on a sensitive subject—a controversial project sponsored by the president, for example—wait before you jump to reply. Do you know how the recipient will use your memo? Do you know who else might see it? Is it possible that your memo can be used against you at a later date? If it is not absolutely essential that you put your views in writing, you might share them verbally or simply delay answering until an issue is no longer an issue.

Although there are no hard and fast rules about when to send or not to send a memo, these guidelines should give you a starting point. At the very least, they should cause you to think about your own habits as a memo writer.

MEMOS AND YOUR CAREER

Why bother to become a good memo writer? There are several reasons. Memos are one of the most personally revealing of all forms of business communication. Only the telephone and face-to-face conversation are more revealing. Each time you write a memo you are (a) showing your skill at putting thoughts in writing; (b) facilitating communications between yourself and others—both vertically and horizontally in the organization; (c) revealing what kind of person you are—your thinking, manner of expression, and areas of strength (and weakness).

Although you are not likely to make or break a career on the basis of one memo, over time your messages will show a pattern. For instance, they will indicate whether you are knowledgeable, have a sense of humor, think clearly — or whether you are uninformed, somewhat stuffy, and muddled.

The time you take to learn how to write concise, effective memos can yield ample benefits over the course of your career. Memos can help to build your reputation in several ways.

Learn to Become a "Great Communicator"

One of the major obstacles to smooth operations in a company is lack of communication between managers and staff. Your well-written memos can keep your boss or colleagues up to date on your work *as it relates to their departments or position*. This point is important — they need to know how your work is important to them, not just to you. You can send periodic progress reports, mention achievement of objectives, point out potential problems, and commend good work.

One project editor at a publishing firm found that over time she had less and less contact with the managing editor, who traveled out of town often. Because she needed to move ahead on her book projects, she sent weekly progress reports to the manager, asking questions if she needed a decision from him. The manager appreciated being kept up to date on her work and could answer her questions either by phone or in writing. She soon gained a reputation as one of the most well-organized editors in the firm.

Memos also act like the nervous system of a company, keeping everyone informed of meetings, changes in company policy, company events, management actions, employee news, and the like. Poorly written memos on these topics can cause a disproportionate amount of misunderstanding and ill will. For example, one memo that circulated in a travel agency made it sound as if insurance coverage for spouses was being reduced when in fact only the deductible figure was changing. The ability to write clear, concise memos on a wide range of so-called routine topics is a highly valued skill in most companies.

Build a Reputation as an Expert

The memo gives you a chance to showcase your knowledge or to become known as an expert in your field. When you have an idea or see a product, opportunity, or important piece of information that your company should know about, you may want to write a memo on the subject and circulate it to the proper people in your firm. For example, you may have an idea for restructuring the company's debt load, or changing its market research strategies, or upgrading office telecommunications equipment.

Not all of your ideas will be accepted, but you can gain a reputation as someone who anticipates trends in the field and finds ways to apply them to the company's situation.

Become an Information Manager

You can also perform a valuable service by developing the skill to extract and present essential information from a glut of data. Computers have made a staggering amount of data available to company personnel — literally at the touch of a button. But human beings must still sift through all the information to determine what it means and why it's important to the company. If you gain the reputation of being able to condense or summarize data from a flood of information, you can greatly increase your value to the company.

One food service firm, for example, received over 300 pages of demographic data each week correlating product sales with various consumer groups. The marketing research manager devised a method of interpreting the trends and explaining in a memo what the information meant in terms of the company's major product lines. His memos enabled the company to adjust its marketing tactics more quickly in response to changing customer tastes.

Protect Yourself Politically

Finally, knowing when and how to write memos can help you to protect your career in politically sensitive situations. A written record of meetings, conversations, actions taken or decisions made, ideas you have had, or disagreements that have arisen with other managers or staff can be well worth the time it takes to put it in writing. Always keep a printed copy of your computer memos; computer files are vulnerable to tampering and to technical problems that can erase or damage a file.

Your memos are your personal representatives to colleagues, staff, and top management. They speak for you and your ideas. It makes sense to have them be the best representatives possible.

Anyone who is willing to learn can write memos well. It's a matter of knowing how to use your strengths and weaknesses to their best advantage. In the next chapter we take a look at some of the common mistakes that plague most memo writers and discuss a new approach for writing effective memos.

SUMMARY

■ Memos are meant to inform, to persuade, and above all to communicate to satisfy the *reader's needs* and the *writer's purpose*.

■ The written word has several advantages over the spoken word:
  — You have an opportunity to think through your message.
  — The reader can consider your message at leisure.
  — You can supplement your written message with diagrams, charts, illustrations, and other materials.
  — Written messages can be filed away "for the record."

■ Each manager or staff member has a personal communications network in the company. Your role and function within the company will determine your communication needs with each group and whether you communicate (a) in person, (b) through electronic means, or (c) through the written word.

■ Memos are generally the best communication choice when
  — You need to reach many people with the same message.
  — You have regular reports to send to the same people.
  — You want to summarize or emphasize information that can be useful to your readers.
  — You wish to send personal messages to individuals or groups.
  — You want to stimulate thinking or action in individuals or groups.
  — The timing or political climate is right.

■ Memos usually should *not* be sent when
  — Person-to-person communication serves your purposes better.
  — You have nothing pertinent to say.
  — Your emotions are running too high.
  — You have more important duties.
  — Broad-based criticism is unwarranted.
  — The timing or political climate is wrong.

■ Memos are among the most personally revealing of all forms of business communication. Each time you write a memo you
- Show your skill at putting thoughts in writing.
- Facilitate communications between you and others in the organization.
- Reveal what kind of person you are.

■ By learning how to write effective memos you can build your reputation in the company several ways. You can
- Become a "great communicator."
- Build a reputation as an expert.
- Become an information manager.
- Protect yourself politically.

CHAPTER TWO

CREATING AN EFFECTIVE MEMO

▼

How would you react to the following memo if you were one of the division managers?

To: All division managers

From: Alice Fisher, Vice President

Subject: Documentation

Although word-of-mouth is a great way to spread a rumor, it's not the best means of conducting business in our divisoin. Once again we have an ongoing disagreement about a budget expenditure because someone gave their approval verbally rather than in writing. After the last disaster, I thought everyone knew better, but this is apparently not the case.

As a result, what should have been a minor issue is getting way out of hand. I want all managers to make sure they get decisions in writing to prevent this kind of misshap in the future. Pass this directive along to your supervisors. Let's not have another dispute over what someone may or may not have *said*. Put it in writing!

If the vice president believes this memo will change things significantly in her division, she would be wise not to bet on it. The memo has

13

all the earmarks of something written in the heat of emotion—a perfect example of when not to write a memo.

But there are other problems that illustrate some of the more common pitfalls and hazards of memo writing. First, the subject line gives no real idea of the memo's purpose. "Documentation" is too broad a category.

Second, the first paragraph, which should announce the purpose, simply describes the situation—a disagreement about a budget expenditure because of a lack of documentation. At this stage, the reader still doesn't know what is the point of the memo. Third, the memo is confusing. What's the "minor issue" that's getting out of hand, the budget disagreement or the lack of documentation?

Fourth, the memo offers no guidance to solve the problem. What, specifically, should the managers do to ensure documentation? What do they tell their supervisors? What situations require documentation? Does a handwritten note qualify or should all documentation be officially typed and signed? The managers will now have to talk to the vice president to find out exactly what she wants done to ensure better documentation. She could have cut short the process by spelling out documentation procedures for the division.

Finally, the memo contains spelling errors ("divisoin," "misshap"), which should have been caught. Such typos simply add to the failure of this piece as communication.

This memo is only one example of several common errors committed by memo writers. We examine the most troublesome of these in the section following. It can be enlightening to examine the memos you have sent and received in light of these pitfalls and hazards.

CHECKLIST OF PITFALLS AND HAZARDS

You can run a quick analysis of your own memo-writing skills by answering the following questions:

1. Do people complain about the chronic lateness of your memos containing key information (dates and times of meetings, ordering information, announcements, etc.)?
2. Do they often have to ask for an explanation of your memos (they don't know what the point of the memo is, or what action they are supposed to take, or what is being asked of them)?

3. Do they frequently need to ask for additional information (sales figures, times or places of meetings, supporting data, etc.)?

4. Do you find yourself following up your memos with telephone calls to give information that should have been included in the written message (e.g., the telephone number of a sales contact, the discount rate on quantity orders, one of the conditions a client has stipulated to close a deal)?

5. Can you usually succeed in selling your ideas through memos or do you have trouble doing so? (E.g., Do people fail to grasp your ideas or their implications? Have you made it clear how they can benefit from adopting your ideas?)

6. Do you send too many memos on the same subject?

7. Are you sending routine memos that no longer serve any purpose?

8. Are you using memos in situations where another form of communication would be better?

If you find yourself answering "yes" to a number of these questions — relax. Most people who write memos are often guilty of these offenses.

In reality, a few common problems are responsible for most of the miscommunication, or lack of communication, that occurs between sender and receiver. They include poor organization, unclear writing, garbled or misleading facts, difficult subject matter, poor delegation or review, and overcommunication.

Poor Organization

One memo in a pharmaceutical firm started out:

> When this company was first founded, the owners couldn't have foreseen the rapid growth in molecular biology that has taken place in the last ten years.

The historical reminiscence went on for another half page before the writer finally got around to the main point — an announcement that the firm had acquired a biogenetics research company.

Because a memo is brief, it must start out with the main point, like a newspaper story. This style of organization is known as an "inverted pyramid," as shown in Exhibit 2–1. Once you have stated the main idea, subsequent information should support, explain, elaborate, or qualify the idea and its meaning for the reader. The information should be

Exhibit 2–1. Inverted Pyramid Structure

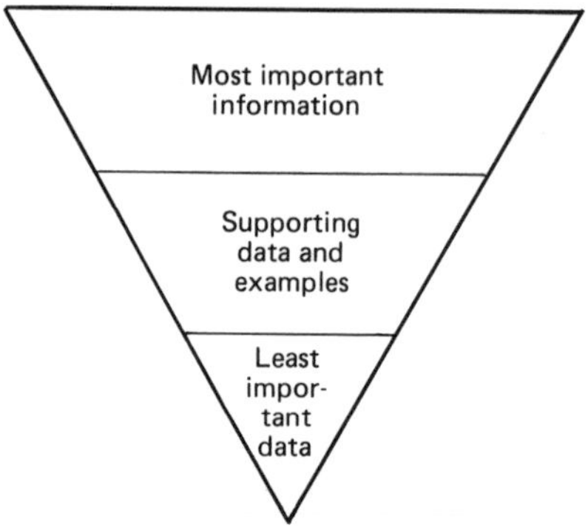

Most important
information

Supporting
data and
examples

Least
impor-
tant
data

given in a logical progression without skipping steps or jumping from one fact to another. Even in a message as mundane as announcing the company picnic, the important information — time, place, and date — should be in the first paragraph, with other details following. (More on how to organize your memos quickly will be found in Chapter 3.)

Unclear Writing

Unclear writing runs a close second to lack of organization as a prime cause of miscommunication. Unclear writing covers not only muddled expressions but the use of "bureaucratese" and jargon as well. One memo touched off a major storm in a manufacturing company when it announced:

> The company will rehabilitate its South Fork and Weston
> plants in the fall.

Because many people were unfamiliar with the term *rehabilitate*, they thought the company meant to close the plants, forcing nearly 4,000 people out of a job. A second memo reassured the employees that the plants were to be renovated, not closed.

Use of bureaucratese in memos is typical of large organizations, such as the government, when they must notify someone of something. However, even small companies can be guilty of this offense. This form of unclear writing explains simple matters in highly complex language. In one instance a government agency sent the following memo to dairy farmers:

It has been determined that bovine feces, under humid or wet conditions, assumes the form of a viscous sludge that constitutes a hazard on wooden or concrete floors. It is recommended that operators periodically clean their floors to prevent accidents.

All these words just to tell dairy farmers that wet manure is slippery on barn floors! The campaign to use plain English in bureaucratic writing hasn't been won yet, but as a memo writer, you can align yourself on the side of clarity.

The use of jargon, except from one knowledgeable professional to another, nearly always confuses rather than enlightens readers. The personnel director of one company sent a memo to all employees that read:

In accordance with our insurance provisions, we must refer any employee ticketed for a DUI traffic offense to a qualified treatment program.

About half of the employees called in to ask what "DUI" (driving under the influence) meant. Because they couldn't understand the message, they couldn't tell if they might fall into the category.

In some cases a simple solution to unclear writing is to have someone else read your memos before you send them out. This precaution gives you a chance to clarify any ambiguous, confusing, or unfamiliar terms or passages.

Misleading or Garbled Facts

The employees of a company that did public opinion surveys for the Department of Defense came to work one morning and found the following memo waiting on their desks:

> Executive Order 324 requires employees working in military estab-
> lishments or in companies who contract with the Department of
> Defense to submit to random drug testing. This company will comply
> with the order, and employees will be tested at random beginning with
> the first of next month.

By 9:05 A.M., the personnel director's phone was ringing off the hook as irate employees from all areas in the company wanted to know why they had to be tested. They did not handle any sensitive or classified documents, manufacture any military materiél, or run equipment that could endanger their lives or the lives of others if mishandled.

The manager who had written the message discovered to his chagrin that he had failed to read the executive order carefully enough. Tucked into its bureaucratic wording was the phrase "all employees GS-*4 level or higher*" would be required to submit to testing. Employees in the manager's firm had all been classified GS-3 or lower. Although the misunderstanding was cleared up, it took three days before the company settled back to normal.

Sweeping generalizations, exaggerations, careless statements, and outright errors can generate a lot of friction between sender and receiver. It costs companies time and money to correct mistakes or misunderstandings. The time you take to check your facts is time invested in clear, effective communication.

Poor Delegation or Review

In most cases, delegating routine memo writing to subordinates is perfectly acceptable. There's no reason why a busy manager or executive should not be relieved of such duties. But when more sensitive, complex, or technical material is involved, it's the manager's reputation that is on the line.

One manager of a major bank delegated some of her memo-writing duties to her new assistant. As long as the memos were short announcements about such matters as meetings or changes in staff schedules, all went well. Then it came time to write a memo about changes in collateral requirements. Delegating the assignment to her assistant turned out to be a mistake. The memo, sent out over the manager's signature, ended up confusing all the lending officers. The embarrassed manager realized she would have to reassume some of her memo-writing duties where more technical matters were concerned.

Unless you can delegate such memo-writing responsibilities with utter confidence, it is best either to do the writing yourself or at least to supervise the person who is writing for you.

The same principle applies when it comes to reviewing your memos: it's your reputation at stake when you send out your messages. Misspellings, grammatical mistakes, and careless errors all reflect on your credibility and judgment. One manager discovered this fact the hard way. He sent out a memo describing a management seminar to be given after hours at the company. As he walked past a few offices, he noticed people chuckling over his memo. When he reread the message, he discovered why. He had written:

> I am pleased to announce that on Tuesday, March 7, at 5:30 pm in the Conference Room, Mr. Roderick Wade and Ms. Constance Burnett will present a seminar on "Exploring Your Personal and Corporate Valves."

The topic was exploring "values," not "valves." A simple mistake, but one that the manager didn't live down for some time.

It's a wise precaution to reread your memos before you send them out — or have someone else review them to check for errors. You want to be remembered for other qualities than being the source of amusing — or irritating — mistakes.

Difficult Subject Matter

Some subjects, such as complicated formulations or technical matters, are not easily captured in words. In one instance, an automotive manufacturing firm had a problem with the steering mechanisms on one particular model. The engineering department analyzed the problem and sent a detailed memo report that the nontechnical sales staff found hard to understand. It wasn't until the chief engineer sent along photographs and diagrams that the meaning became clear.

If you have to describe difficult subject matter, don't depend on words alone to convey the message. Sketches, computer graphics, photographs, or other explanatory and illustrative materials can help to get your message across to the reader.

Overcommunication — The Paper Blizzard

Too much communication can be just as bad as too little. Particularly now that computers make sending memos so easy, the communications logjam in some companies has become a real problem. Unnecessary memos are a drain on everyone's time and should be eliminated. The following are ways in which people contribute to the problem:

1. They write memos that shouldn't be written in the first place. Do you really need to flash a memo on someone's computer screen asking them to come and see you? It may be quicker than a phone call (you save a few seconds time punching in the person's extension), but it also interrupts someone's work on the terminal. A phone call may be more appropriate.

2. They send copies to everyone rather than think through who really needs to receive the message. If you're afraid you may offend someone by skipping them, consider that people who receive unwanted memos are just as likely to be upset at the interruption.

3. They use memos as a way of tooting their own horn. Managers may want to let people know, under the guise of official business, about an achievement that makes them look good. Unfortunately, such efforts tend to be rather transparent.

Excessive paperwork wastes time at the sending and receiving end and should be fought vigorously. One way to combat the paper blizzard is to ask yourself, "Is this memo necessary?" Use the criteria described in Chapter 1 as a guide. If the answer is "no," you've saved yourself time and effort.

Another way to streamline communications is to cut down on the number of copies distributed. For memos that are circulated by routing list, you might attach a slip that gives recipients a choice of remaining on the list or of having their name removed from it. In that way, the readers can help you to decide who should get the memo and who can be skipped.

A NEW APPROACH TO MEMO WRITING

In the old approach to memo writing, you spend a great deal of time agonizing over how to start, what to say, and how to say it. Or, at the other extreme, you dash off a memo that may leave out key facts, confuse the reader, and fail as a piece of communication. The needs of both sender and receiver are often lost in the process.

Even books on how to improve your writing may not be much help when it comes to memos. They fail to take into account that often you don't have time to do detailed outlining or revising. You need to get the memo organized and written quickly and effectively on the first or second try—certainly by the third—with only minor revisions for grammar, spelling, and style.

Three Steps in Memo Writing

The new approach to memo writing involves learning key strategies that can help you to write effective memos quickly, without loss of meaning or impact. In the chapters that follow, we show you how to do most of the work *before* you put your thoughts on paper (or computer screen) so that you spend the minimum amount of time writing and revising. These strategies can keep you from getting stuck at any point in the process.

We begin by breaking down memo writing into three steps:

- Preparation—determining the purpose, topic, and reader's needs the memo serves
- Writing—organizing and writing
- Review—revising and checking the memo

These steps work just as well for a one- to two-page memo as they do for a 20-page memo report. Once you learn these steps, you will always know how to start your memo, organize it, and write it quickly.

Step One: Preparation.   All memo writing can be boiled down to the process of answering four key questions:

1. What is the purpose or point of this message—why am I writing it?
2. Who is the audience—whom do I want to inform or influence?
3. What is the scope and meaning of my message—what do the readers *need* to know versus what is just *nice* to know? What does the message *mean* to them?

4. What action or response do I want from the readers?

If you can answer these questions in one or two sentences each before you start writing, the job is nearly half finished. These questions also can be used in the writing stage to help you stay on target and in the review stage to make sure you have answered the questions completely.

Preparation strategies, discussed in Chapter 3, are designed to help you answer the four questions by enlisting your creative powers — your "right brain" capacities — as well as your analytical powers. By using such techniques as dialogue and mapping, you can answer the key questions in surprisingly little time. These techniques take advantage of the brain's natural tendency to organize the data it receives.

Preparation also involves gathering any background or supporting data you will need to write your memo and deciding who should receive copies.

Step Two: Writing. Even after you have successfully negotiated the first hurdle, you may find yourself balking at the writing stage. Writing strategies, discussed in Chapter 4, are geared to help you think as you write. In many instance, people suffer from the paralyzing expectation that their memos must be perfect, or more important or official sounding, than their other communications. As a result, they lose their own "voice" and adopt a stiff, unnatural style that confuses rather than communicates.

Writing can be as natural as speaking. In Chapter 4 we show you how to use tone, active language, paragraphing, and other devices to convey your message and to meet your readers' needs. We also discuss various writing formulas that can be used to help you organize your memo more rapidly. You can use the four key questions to help you stay focused on the purpose of your message. At this stage you can determine what attachments or illustrations, if any, your message might need.

Step Three: Review. In the review stage, you apply the finishing touches to your writing. This step offers you the opportunity to take a final look through your memo before it goes out with your name on it. Have you answered the four questions adequately?

You will need to double-check facts, names, dates, and so on, and check for grammar and spelling mistakes. Make sure you delete all excess words and inflated terminology. You can also take another look at your distribution list and add or subtract any names.

Remember, your purpose is not to write the perfect memo —

although that may happen. Your purpose is to write accurate, effective communication that gets the results you want.

Let's take another look at the memo that opened the chapter. Here's how it might read if Alice Fisher had used the new approach.

To: All division managers

From: Alice Fisher, Vice President

Subject: Guidelines for Improving Documentation

I am asking your help to improve written documentation of our division's activities. Over the past three months alone, we have had several disagreements over expense items that were approved verbally but not in writing. These arguments held up production of a key consumer item.

For the smooth operation of our division, and for your own protection, keep written file copies of all important decisions and actions taken by you and your staff. These include agreements, approvals, solutions to problems, reprimands, commendations, directions, minutes of meetings, and the like.

The form of documentation may vary depending on the circumstances. For most occasions, a typed and signed letter or report is appropriate. In some cases, a handwritten note will be acceptable, provided it is legible and dated. Please make sure your supervisors understand when documentation is necessary and the proper procedures to follow.

If you have any suggestions that would help to streamline the process of documentation, please let me know. I appreciate your help to "get it in writing."

This memo answers the four key questions:

■ What is the point of this memo? (The point is to improve documentation in order to prevent disagreements.)
■ Who is the audience? (Its audience is all division managers and their staff.)

■ What is the scope and meaning of the message? (It is a statement of the problem and its solution in specific terms.)

■ What action or response is required? (It instructs staff to implement the guidelines to document important decisions and actions.)

Both the sender and receiver have a much clearer understanding of what they can do about the problem. The memo also seeks to elicit cooperation and not to dictate a vague policy that no one can implement.

In the next chapter we show you a few key strategies for the first step—"Preparation"—in creating an effective memo.

SUMMARY

■ The following questions can help you quickly analyze your memo-writing skills:

— Do people complain about the chronic lateness of your memos containing key information?

— Do they often have to ask for an explanation of your memos?

— Do they frequently need to ask for additional information?

— Do you find yourself following up your memos with telephone calls to give information that should have been included in the written message?

— Can you usually succeed in selling your ideas through memos or do you have trouble doing so?

— Do you send too many memos on the same subject?

— Are you sending routine memos that no longer serve any purpose?

— Are you using memos in situations where another form of communication would serve better?

■ The most common pitfalls and hazards of memo writing are caused by a few basic problems—poor organization, unclear writing, garbled or misleading facts, difficult subject matter, poor delegation or review, and overcommunication.

■ A new approach to memo writing breaks the process down into three steps: preparation, writing, review.

■ *Preparation*
   — Answer the four key questions. (What is the purpose or point of this message? Who is the audience? What is the scope and meaning of my message? What action or response do I want from the readers?)
   — Conduct background research and decide who will receive copies.
   — Organize data and select appropriate structure.
■ *Writing*
   — Write the first draft.
   — Select any attachments or illustrations.
■ *Review*
   — Edit and revise draft for clarity, accuracy, brevity.
   — Check for errors in grammar, spelling, facts, and so on.
   — Make final check of distribution list.

PREPARATION

HOW TO START

▼

Geri Towers slumped into her chair and stared at her blank terminal, her face a picture of despair. Paul looked up from the next desk.

"What's the matter?" he asked.

"I found this great software to improve our accounting procedures. Mr. Grant told me to write up the details in a memo by Friday. *This* Friday!" She gestured at the pile of manufacturer literature and computer journals that littered her desk. Geri could feel her stomach tighten in fear.

"How am I supposed to get a memo written in two days? Where do I start?"

GERI'S DILEMMA is all too familiar to many managers and staff. They often have to write memos under considerable pressure that must convince someone to take a particular action or to respond in a particular way.

The basic principle in writing under pressure is *to have a variety of strategies to work through problems at any point.* If one method doesn't work, you can choose another. With these strategies, you always have a way around any writing block.

Many people find that getting started is the most difficult, intimidating part of any writing task. Actually there's a well-defined pathway you can follow, regardless of the type of memo you have to write. Keeping the four key questions in mind, you should

- State your purpose and define what action or response you want.
- Analyze your readers.

- Know your topic—determine its scope and meaning.
- Plan and organize your memo.

By working on these steps, you are giving your mind something constructive to do to get past the anxiety. The important point is not to battle "fear of writing" but to outmaneuver it by breaking the task into smaller, manageable steps. Once you begin working, the anxiety generally subsides on its own.

STATE YOUR PURPOSE AND THE RESPONSE YOU WANT

Why are you writing this memo? What do you want from your readers? The answers to these two questions may be as simple as "I want to announce a change in company parking regulations, and I want the readers to understand and comply with the changes." Or they may be as complex as "I want to convince top management that the proposed merger with Omni will put us too deeply in debt. I want them to reject or seriously to reconsider this course of action."

Jot down your purpose and the response you want in one or two sentences. If you find yourself unable to answer these two questions in writing, try a strategy known as "dialoguing."

 ## WRITING STRATEGY 1: DIALOGUING

The basic principle in this strategy is to set up a "dialogue" between yourself and the intended recipient(s) of the memo to help you define your purpose and the response you want. You can either use another person as a stand-in for the reader or carry on an imaginary dialogue.

This strategy frees you from the tyranny of the written word and allows your mind access to a wider range of knowledge you may not know you possess. Often people aren't aware of what they know until they hear themselves say it.

If you talk over the purpose with someone else, have them put themselves in your reader's shoes as much as possible. In

Geri's case, for example, her colleague, Paul, asks questions from Mr. Grant's point of view.

GERI: I've got something to tell you about the new accounting software called PAYWRITE.

PAUL: Okay, I've got about five minutes to spare. Go!

GERI: Well, I've researched five major accounting programs and they all take up at least 360K in memory just to run their . . .

PAUL: Wait! I haven't got time to hear about these other programs. What about PAYWRITE?

GERI: I'm getting to that.

PAUL: No, start with it. You've just used up two minutes telling me something I don't need to know. I'm interested in what PAYWRITE will do for us.

GERI: It has a graphics program that's more powerful than the one we're using, its data base can handle more variables . . .

PAUL: So it's the greatest program ever—what will it *do* for us?

GERI: It will solve several major problems in accounting, particularly calculating year-end profits, foreign debt, and a breakdown of sales by region for our branch offices. It can do this faster than other programs, using less memory. You get more bang for the buck.

PAUL: Now you're talking. So what do you want from me?

GERI: Purchase PAYWRITE and fund a training program for the accounting staff.

Geri has hit on the purpose of her memo—telling her boss how PAYWRITE will solve the firm's accounting problems. The purpose is not to describe how she found the right software or simply to list PAYWRITE's features. The purpose is to focus on results—how PAYWRITE can solve our problems. This topic is sure to capture the attention of her harried boss.

Geri has also discovered what response she wants—her boss should buy the software and pay for employee training. She can sell her boss on PAYWRITE's training program in her memo.

This short dialogue has prevented her from starting out with the wrong approach. Her natural tendency, as is the case with many people, is to begin with less important information and build up to the main point. In a memo, you generally lead with your main point. Thus, even if the reader is interrupted after the first sentence or paragraph, he or she will still know the purpose of your memo.

If you use an imaginary dialogue, try to visualize your reader as vividly as possible, capturing the individual's personality and interests. You might feel a little strange at first hearing voices in your head. But you'll find that playing devil's advocate with yourself can cut down on the time it takes to define your purpose and determine what you want from the reader.

KNOW YOUR READERS

Because true communication fulfills the reader's needs as well as the writer's purpose, you need to know something about your readers. This means learning about their personal characteristics and, in general, what motivates them. Such knowledge can help you to set the scope and tone of your memo. If you can identify with your readers, you have a better chance of writing a memo that engages their attention and cooperation.

Personal Characteristics

The easiest place to start is with some of the more obvious personal characteristics of your readers—their gender, age, knowledge, and position.

Gender. The key word here is *inclusion*. Make sure when you address a memo to a group—whether it consists of clerical workers, staff, managers, or executives—you have included men and women. Today more women are entering middle and upper management and more men are found in previously all-women positions, such as support staff or assistants. You cannot assume that "secretary" automatically means "she" or "CEO" automatically means "he."

Also, avoid thinking in stereotypes if you are sending a memo to a man or woman in the company. In one firm, the purchasing agent sent a memo to a female manager about a new copier. He omitted the technical details, assuming she would not be interested in such information because she was a woman. In fact, she had sold copiers before coming to the firm and knew the technical details inside out. She had to ask for more information before she could make a decision about buying that particular model. The purchasing agent learned a valuable lesson: never make assumptions strictly on the basis of gender.

If the group you are writing to is all female or all male, again, resist the temptation to treat the two genders like two different species. Try to understand their needs from their points of view to avoid using an inappropriate tone—for example, condescending or too stiff and formal. Have someone else read the memo to determine whether you have addressed the group appropriately.

Age.   Write to bridge the generation gap—don't use language or references from one era to appeal to people of another era. Someone who grew up in the 1960s, for example, would understand a reference to the "Woodstock generation," but it's doubtful that someone who came of age in the 1950s or 1970s would have quite the same appreciation of the term. Likewise, if you use phrases from your teenage children in your memos, you shouldn't be surprised if your adult colleagues take you less than seriously.

Word choice is important in projecting a mature, in-charge image of yourself in your memos. If you are a young manager trying to motivate older employees to greater efforts, pitch your language to their level. One young manager in a manufacturing plant wrote the following memo to his line workers:

> We need more hustle on the production line if we're going to go over the top on the quota this month. We can't let equipment problems slow us down. I've checked out the figures from the previous quarter, and we're down by 10% for the same period this quarter. We still have time to bring up our production level. Let's go for it—we can pull this off if we all work together!!!

The line workers' reaction to this memo was, "Who is this guy kidding?" They felt that the tone of the memo was juvenile and that the manager had failed to appreciate the effect of faulty equipment on production work. A more effective memo, written to appeal to the employees' needs, might go as follows:

> Over the past month, we have experienced a general slowdown in production on the day shift. Part of the problem was due to a faulty conveyor belt, which has been fixed. I know that the day shift has the best record in the company for meeting production quotas. I feel confident that we can make up the slack in production if we all pull together. If you have any suggestions about how to speed up the line work, pass them on to my office.

This memo makes the problem—and solution—a team effort. It recognizes past good work, appeals to the workers' pride, and urges them to greater efforts. The tone and language level of this memo create a bridge between a younger manager and older workers.

Knowledge. The educational level of your readers and the knowledge of your subject that they possess will have a direct bearing on how you address them in your memo. You want to avoid the dual traps of talking down to your readers or talking over their heads. Even in the same company, people speak different occupational languages.

A corporate lawyer, for example, would be able to understand a complex, technical memo describing applications of tax law to various overseas ventures. On the other hand, the sales manager or the vice president of the division probably would be lost reading the same memo. They would want to know what difference the tax law will make to them—will it mean a change in pricing structure, accounting methods, the way in which earnings are reported, and so on?

If you are writing a memo to a group in which the knowledge levels vary, you have two choices: you can split the group and write specific memos to each subgroup, or you can compose a general message aimed at the least knowledgeable of the group's members. If you choose the second option, make sure to keep your language clear and straightforward. That way you neither offend nor confuse your readers. The following memo was written to the lawyers and clerical staff in a corporation's legal department.

> Enclosed is a copy of the new corporate contract form to be used for doing business with independent consultants and subcontractors.

Please note that all negotiated changes to the contract must be typewritten as an addendum rather than written into the text of the contract. The addendum must be signed by all parties to the contract.

Clerical staff should ensure that all required signatures appear both on the last page of the contract and on the addendum before the contract is mailed and filed.

In the same vein, don't assume that readers with academic degrees must be addressed in sophisticated, academic language. Most professionals — whether doctors, lawyers, executives, scientists, or other specialists — appreciate communications that are clear, concise, and accurate. If they want academic language, they can turn to their professional books and journals.

Position.   Take the time to verify the formal position and title of your reader(s). This knowledge can influence the tone you adopt in your memo. For example, your memo to a colleague can be informal, more like direct conversation between equals. Addressing a superior, however, calls for a more formal tone. Your writing should be free from overly familiar remarks or references. The two examples below illustrate how two requests, one sent to a colleague in research and development and one to the R & D vice president, would be worded.

To: Bob Patton, R & D
From: Irene Vandanowitz
Subject: LASER-CUT SILICON WAFERS

Bob, I heard through the grapevine that you have perfected a way to laser-cut silicon wafers to the specifications we need. We're working on a new microchip that is six times smaller than our Micro S7 chip. Could you cut a test series for us next week? Call me at x437.

To: Yuri Ammon, Vice President, R & D
From: Irene Vandanowitz, Supervisor, Design Engineering
Subject: LASER-CUT SILICON WAFERS

Our department is currently working on a new microchip only one-sixth the size of the Micro S7 chip. We understand that your department has perfected a means to laser-cut silicon wafers to the specifications we need.

We would like very much to arrange for your department to cut a test series of our new microchip design next week. Please call me at ext. 437 at your earliest convenience to discuss a possible time and date.

The first memo between two colleagues dispenses with formality and states a simple request. The language is more casual and cuts easily across departmental boundaries. The second memo reflects the difference in rank between the sender and receiver. The sender acknowledges the receiver's authority and frames the request so that departmental boundaries are strictly observed.

What Motivates Readers

Knowing some of the personal characteristics of your readers will give you a general profile of your audience. Knowing what motivates them will bring that profile to life and help you to decide what tone to adopt and how to get the results you want.

The following list highlights some of the more common concerns that motivate people in business:

Convenience	saving time, increasing efficiency
Profit	improving it
Saving	spending less
Productivity	increasing it
Prestige	position and pride
Loyalty	fidelity to others and one's self
Security	confidence in the future
Health	maintaining or improving it
Curiosity	a sense of wonder, a willingness to take risks

You can probably add to the list, but these motivators are a good place to start.

For example, the memo that Geri has to write (in the chapter opener) can be slanted differently depending on what motivates her boss, Mr. Grant. Although most people are motivated by several concerns, in general, one is predominant. If Grant is motivated primarily by

■ Saving—Geri can emphasize in what ways the software will reduce labor and processing costs and justify its price.

■ Convenience — she can emphasize how the software will make the computer network easier and faster, how it can improve compatibility among different terminals, and so on.

■ Prestige — she can emphasize how executives at his level need to have the most effective computer power at their command; also, if appropriate, she can mention other top firms that use the new software.

■ Productivity — she can emphasize that the software can do more functions simultaneously or run programs faster, thus increasing the amount of computer time available to each employee.

Thus, while the memo in each case will contain virtually the same information about the software program, Geri can slant the data to capture the attention and interest of her boss. She is accomplishing two goals: (a) showing sensitivity to her boss's problems, concerns, and needs; and (b) ensuring that her memo has the best possible chance of making an impact.

If you are unfamiliar with the characteristics of your readers, find out from others what they are like. A few minutes spent researching your recipients can mean the difference between a memo that's read and one that's tossed aside or ignored.

You can construct a quick checklist of reader characteristics, as shown in Table 3—1. This matrix can help you create an audience profile for any particular memo.

Table 3—1. Reader Profile — Brief Sketch

Characteristics	Comments
Gender	
Age	
Knowledge	
Position	
Other traits	
Major motivators	

KNOW YOUR TOPIC: DETERMINE
ITS SCOPE AND MEANING

The purpose of your memo, the response you want, and your reader profile will help you to determine what you should cover in your memo. In Geri's case, for example, most of her memo will be devoted to describing features of PAYWRITE that solve the major problems in accounting. She doesn't need to describe how well the program works on other computer systems that the firm doesn't own. She is separating what her reader *needs* to know from what is simply *nice* to know.

When you determine the scope and meaning of your topic, you are, in effect, selecting what you will discuss from a whole range of possible facts and figures. The purpose, response, and reader profile act as a framework for the rest of your memo. They give you a criteria by which to judge whether the information you are including in the memo supports its main purpose.

This stage is the first step in planning and organizing your memo. Four strategies can help you to determine the scope and meaning of your topic: laundry list, mapping, freewriting, and dialoguing.

Laundry List

The "laundry list" technique is a way to brainstorm ideas about your memo topic in a very short time. Once you've generated the list, you can choose the items that belong in your memo and use them to create an outline.

 ## WRITING STRATEGY 2: LAUNDRY LIST

The principle behind this strategy is to free your mind from preconceptions regarding what the memo "should" be about. This involves a brainstorming session, and all ideas are fair game. Simply jot down a list of items that come to mind, regardless of how trivial or irrelevant they may appear to be. Don't edit your thoughts or second-guess yourself. You can always eliminate items when you create the final outline or plan.

Suppose, for example, you must write a memo explaining to your staff how a recent departmental reorganization will affect them. You've identified your purpose, to "explain the reorganization

and how it will improve employee productivity and documentation."
You want your readers to "understand and cooperate with the
changes." Now you need to determine the scope of your topic.
Your laundry list might look like the following:

Departmental Reorganization
1. Consolidate two jobs — sales manager and marketing
manager — into one, manager of sales and marketing.
2. Streamline end-of-week reports on sales and worker
productivity.
3. Eliminate confusion about what is responsibility of sales
and what is responsibility of marketing.
4. Open office area — make it look less cluttered.
5. Make it easier for employees to know who's in charge of
what functions.
6. Make it easier for me to pass along departmental
information to higher management.
7. Address employee concerns about their own jobs and
responsibilities:
   — Show them how their jobs will change, how they will
   stay the same.
   — Ask for their cooperation and suggestions — emphasize
   the need to pull together as a team.
8. Address rumors that staff will be let go:
   — Only one management position will be eliminated —
   that person will be relocated within company.
   — No support staff will be let go or replaced.
9. Relay redecorating scheme — new carpet, new paint job,
modular furniture.
10. Tell how reorganization can open up career opportunities
for some employees if they are willing to educate themselves.

Looking over the laundry list, you can see that some items can be
eliminated, such as Item 4, "Opens office area — makes it look less
cluttered." A better way to cover the issue of office space turns up
in Item 9, in which you list what will be done to improve employees'
working environment. Other items, such as 3 and 5, are really
variations on the same idea — clarification of responsibilities and
reporting relationships. These two ideas can be combined in your
final outline.

Some items may be marginal, such as Item 6. Do employees need to know your job will be easier, and if so, how it will affect them? You may want to make the item relate more directly to employee concerns. If you can pass information along more easily to higher management, does that include their suggestions and comments?

Review the list to see if you have forgotten any topic. Will the reorganization have any effect on the way salary increases are calculated, for example? What about vacation schedules, overtime, and the other perquisites that employees are likely to be concerned about? Your revised list might look like the following:

Revised List—Departmental Reorganization

1. Explain basics of departmental reorganization:
    — It consolidates sales manager and marketing manager into manager, sales and marketing.
    — All employees now report to one manager—it streamlines day-to-day operations and eliminates confusion over who has what responsibilities.
2. Address employee concerns about job security:
    — No support staff will be let go or replaced.
    — Only one management position will be eliminated—that person will be relocated within company.
    — There will be no changes in salary or commission structure, job duties, benefits, or working hours.
3. Discuss opportunities that reorganization opens up:
    — Employees have greater chance for expanding their jobs.
    — There will be more opportunities to obtain training and work-related education.
4. Mention redecorating plans:
    — There will be new carpeting, a new paint job, modular furniture.
    — Redecorating should make office spaces more functional and convenient.
5. Talk about transition time and need for employee cooperation and suggestions.

When you are using the listing technique to reply to a memo, you may want to jot down the list on the memo itself. This is particularly useful if you must delay writing a reply. When you return to the job, you'll have the memo and your thoughts on one piece of paper. For example, if a memo asks your opinion of a new form for keeping track of inventory, you might note your immediate thoughts on the memo: "Good section for signing materials in and out; not enough room to write in reorders; should be a space for supervisor's initials."

The laundry list technique allows you to tap into your creativity before calling in your critical, analytical mind. Ignore the voices inside that may say, "That's a stupid idea, why are you writing that?" Or, "This is a waste of time — get to work!" If you can put those voices aside and simply allow yourself to brainstorm, you may be surprised and pleased at the ideas your list generates.

Mapping

Mapping, a relatively new technique, is also known as "mindmapping" or "clustering." Some people find this technique easier and more effective to use than listing. This strategy takes advantage of the mind's natural ability to organize information. It seldom organizes according to formal outlining rules — Roman numerals, big and little letters, and the like. On the other hand, neither does the mind store information in a chaotic jumble of facts, impressions, and sensory details. Rather, the unconscious arranges information in a way that mapping can help to reveal.

 ## WRITING STRATEGY 3: MAPPING

Although there is no one correct way to do mapping, there are some general guidelines that work.

1. Write the topic of your memo in the center of a piece of paper. For example, "departmental reorganization" or, in Geri's case, "PAYWRITE."
2. Draw a circle or square around the topic. This may seem like an odd step, but for some reason the mind likes to have visual boundaries around a subject.
3. Draw a line branching from the circle or square for every main item or concern you wish to cover. To identify these

items or concerns, you might ask yourself the 5 W's and 1 H of journalism: who, what, when, where, why, and how. Or you might select the topics by section. In Geri's situation, for example, she might choose as main branches "accounting problems solved," "extra features," "training requirements," "cost considerations," "testimonials," and the like.

4. Don't try to organize the branches, just let yourself develop them. Organizing comes later.

5. You can use different colored pens or pencils for different branches. Some people find using different colors makes organizing the memo easier.

Exhibit 3–1 shows how mapping works for the memo Geri has to write about PAYWRITE.

Exhibit 3–1. Example of Mapping Technique

You may find some surprises using this technique. One manager, for example, discovered that in doing a quick mapping for a memo about a new time sheet, he had written "3:00" under the branch titled "Advantages" of the new form. At first he had no idea what the item meant.

Then it came to him that under the old system every Friday at 3:00 P.M. he had to start badgering his staff to turn in their weekly timesheets. He needed to compile their reports for the payroll department before 5:00 P.M. With the new form, all he had to do was collect the sheets at 5:00 P.M. The data processing clerks in payroll would do the calculations via computer. Thus, the new time sheet would remove a major source of irritation between himself and his staff. He included the item in his memo under the subheading "Advantages."

Although your *conscious* mind may not remember such things, your *unconscious* mind will often find a way to call attention to them. That's the value of using a technique that uses all parts of the mind.

Dialoguing

Dialoguing (referred to earlier in the chapter) works as well in this step as it does to help you determine the purpose and response you want. This technique is especially useful if you tend to experience a mental block when it comes to putting your thoughts on paper. Again, the principle is not to butt your head against the block but to find a way around it and to get your creative ideas flowing.

In one instance, a sales manager of a restaurant paper products supplier had to explain to his staff a new method of calculating commissions. All he could think about was how vehemently his staff was going to resist the change. Every time he tried to put something on paper, he drew a blank. Finally, he called in one of his senior salespeople and asked her help in talking him through the memo. Their dialogue went something like the following:

► WRITING STRATEGY 4: DIALOGUING

FRANK	(sales manager): Headquarters has developed a new method of figuring your commissions.
ALICIA	(salesperson): Oh yeah? What's wrong with the old way?
FRANK:	Well ... for one thing it doesn't reflect the changes in our customer base from small restaurants to chain business. (He jots that point down.) For another thing, our sales territory has gotten smaller in the past year. You don't have to spend as much time traveling, so you have fewer expenses to figure into your calculations. (He makes a note of this point.)
ALICIA:	So the bottom line is that with this new system, we'll end up with less money!
FRANK:	No, no! Well ...you might get a little less on the small restaurant sales, but you'll get a *bigger* percentage of the sales to chain restaurants. We want to develop more chain business, so this can act as an incentive. (He writes this point down.)
ALICIA:	Just how complicated is this new method?
FRANK:	The data processing department has written a computer program for it. The whole sales force will be trained in how to use it—you can even program the basic operations into your calculators. (He writes this down.)
ALICIA:	All this sounds great for the guys who have chain clients, but what about those of us who service smaller chains and independent restaurants?
FRANK:	We'll have to work out reassignment details based on sales record and seniority. It may take some time, but I think everyone will benefit in the long haul.

By the end of the dialogue, Frank has his main points to use in the memo. The opportunity to talk it over with someone helped him to overcome his mental block.

Freewriting

Freewriting can help you either to generate ideas or to get a first rough copy after you have done your listing or mapping. It can also help you to loosen up if you find listing or mapping difficult to do. The freewriting strategy is especially useful for short memos.

 WRITING STRATEGY 5: FREEWRITING

The key to freewriting, as in listing or mapping, is to ignore the critic or editor in you who wants to revise or correct your words as you write. Simply start writing—either with a pen or on the computer—without making changes or corrections. For the time being, forget about grammar, spelling, punctuation, organization, or format. All that can be added later. Just write.

Suppose, for example, that you had to explain to a staff member what you wanted done on a particular project.

Freewriting:

Roberta Hong Kingston best person for this job. Background research on Carmine Consolidated—need to profile top management and get a list of their subsidiaries. Particularly Middle East connections. (Gary in legal wanted a check on their possible link to government insider trading investigation in New York.) Make sure financial data is current—Dun & Bradstreet info only up to second quarter. Report needed for next board meeting on Monday.

Revised:

The board is considering the possibility of a major joint venture with Carmine Consolidated. We need an in-depth report on the following:

■ A concise profile of all top management personnel

■ A list and brief description of Carmine's subsidiaries, with particular attention paid to connections in the Middle East

■ A complete analysis of its financial picture — the board members would like current quarter figures where possible

■ An investigation into any possible link between Carmine management and the U.S. government's insider trading investigation in New York

The report is due Monday, December 12, one week before the board meeting on December 19. This will give us time to make any corrections or revisions before presenting the report to the board. I know you will do your usual thorough job.

In general, it's easier to freewrite after you have generated your topic ideas. You can use the ideas to create paragraphs and eventually your memo. You'll need to go back and edit your work, but you have your rough copy. For most people, that means the hardest part is over.

Research Your Topic

The methods described earlier should reveal any gaps in your knowledge that need to be filled before you write the memo. Do you know meeting times and dates? Are you sure about the spelling of client names? Do you need background data on marketing or sales figures? Do you have accurate information on equipment specifications or warranties? If you're asking for a decision from your readers, have you given them all the facts they need?

It's a good idea to do your research before you write the final memo. This prevents you from having to stop writing to look up information. Generally, the more interruptions, the harder it is to finish your memo.

Decide Who Gets Copies

The preparation stage is also a good time to think about who should get copies of your message. In some cases, the decision is simple; for example, for the announcement of a meeting, copies go to each person who should attend. In other cases, however, the decision is not so clear cut. Being included, or left out, of a distribution list can have political as well as practical implications. Use the following questions as guidelines when deciding whom to include on your copies list:

■ Aside from those directly involved, who has an interest, connection, or question regarding the subject of your message?
■ Is there someone new on the management team who needs to be included on your list?
■ Are you including certain individuals as a matter of routine without considering whether the topic is of any interest to them?
■ Does your assistant or supervisor have any suggestions about who should get copies?
■ Should you send blind copies to your boss or to anyone else?

Give your distribution list serious thought before composing your message. Part of effective communications is sending the right memos to the right people.

ORGANIZE YOUR MEMO

There are several formulas you can use to plan and organize your memo after you've done your listing, mapping, or freewriting work. One of the most common, and most effective, ways to organize a memo is to use the *inverted pyramid* structure, mentioned in Chapter 2.

Inverted Pyramid

When using the inverted pyramid structure, you state the most important point first, focus your reader's attention on it, then use the rest of your memo to explain, support, and develop it more fully. This structure works as well for a two-paragraph memo as it does for a multipage memo.

Inductive reasoning. The key to the inverted pyramid is the principle of *inductive reasoning*. This means that you state your conclusion first, then discuss how you arrived at the conclusion and why it should be supported. *Deductive reasoning*, the opposite form, begins with minor points and builds toward the conclusion or climax of a story or message. Although such suspense works well in a novel or a movie, it is not appropriate for a memo. Your readers don't have time to sift through your message looking for the point.

In general, the following order is used in the inverted pyramid format:

- Answers come before explanations
- Requests come before reasons
- Summaries come before details
- Conclusions come before discussions
- General statements come before specifics

Diamond sequence. The exception to this order occurs when you have to say "no" to a request, need to ask for something that the reader doesn't want to give, or must catch the reader up on the history of a situation. In such cases, you may need to prepare the reader by giving your reasons or explanations *before* stating the main point. For example, suppose you were asked to substitute for a speaker and must decline. Your memo might look like the following:

I was flattered to receive your request to fill in as speaker for Sarah Westings at the Founders' Night Banquet. Although I would like very much to say "yes," unfortunately I will be in Los Angeles that night at a business conference. *Therefore I must regretfully decline your invitation.* (Main point of the memo—our emphasis.)

Please keep me in mind for the future, however. I admire your organization's record of community service and would be honored to serve as speaker at a later date.

The structure of such memos resembles a diamond shape. Exhibit 3—2 compares the inverted pyramid and diamond sequences.

Exhibit 3—2. Inverted Pyramid and Diamond Sequences

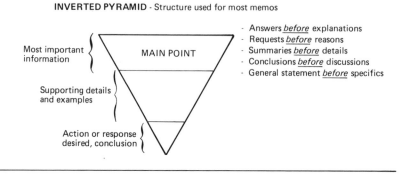

INVERTED PYRAMID - Structure used for most memos

Most important information

MAIN POINT

Supporting details and examples

Action or response desired, conclusion

- Answers *before* explanations
- Requests *before* reasons
- Summaries *before* details
- Conclusions *before* discussions
- General statement *before* specifics

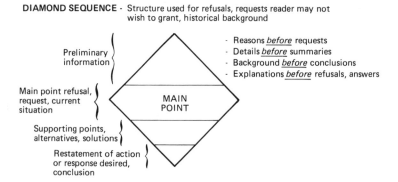

DIAMOND SEQUENCE - Structure used for refusals, requests reader may not wish to grant, historical background

Preliminary information

Main point refusal, request, current situation

MAIN POINT

Supporting points, alternatives, solutions

Restatement of action or response desired, conclusion

- Reasons *before* requests
- Details *before* summaries
- Background *before* conclusions
- Explanations *before* refusals, answers

Ranking topics.   You can use your purpose to help rank your points in order of importance. In the case of the departmental reorganization, for example, you can ask yourself which of the topics you listed are likely to be the most important for employees to know. You can then renumber the items, leading off with the most important one.

If you have trouble identifying the main topic, ask yourself which item you would save if you could keep only one? Put that item in your first paragraph — or your first sentence if appropriate.

If you use the mapping technique, you can number the main branches to indicate the priority of topics, as shown for Geri's mapping in Exhibit 3—3. You can use these topics as headings when you begin to write your memo.

Exhibit 3-3. Example of Mapping Technique-Ranking Topics

In the freewriting method, you can rank topics by circling or numbering the main points and placing them first when you write the final version.

The inverted pyramid structure can be applied to several formats to help you organize your memos. The most widely used formats include problem-solving, cause-and-effect, chronological, question-and-answer, functional, and reporting sequences. Each format is appropriate for slightly different situations.

Problem-solving Format

The problem-solving format generally begins with a description of a problem or problems and concludes with a discussion of solutions. A longer memo might also include an analysis of the problem, but shorter memos stick to the problem—solution sequence.

This structure is particularly useful if you want to persuade your boss or others that you have a solution to a problem facing the company. The problem—solution sequence gives you a chance to show your understanding of the situation and a step-by-step solution. Suppose, for example, one of the graphic artists in your company quits unexpectedly. You state the problem this situation creates and propose your solution.

As you all know, Pam Byrne had to resign her position unexpectedly because of an illness in her family. This leaves us shorthanded with only two weeks left to finish the Hartford annual report. To meet our deadline, even with part-time help, we'll have to take the following steps:

- Postpone the CNA job until mid-April
- Delay work on all nonclient projects, such as the employee newsletter
- Schedule overtime and weekend hours (this is a good time to earn extra pay!)
- Decline any new jobs until the Hartford report is completed

If you have suggestions, let me know. With hard work and a good team effort, we can deliver this project on time!

Cause-and-Effect Format

The cause-and-effect format, which is similar to the problem-solving structure, is used to focus on a current situation that requires immediate action. You can lead off with either the causes of a situation, if they are known, or the effects, depending on what you wish to emphasize. A toxic chemical spill, a series of workplace accidents, or a natural disaster that has affected firm operations are situations that lend themselves to a cause-and-effect format.

The primary purpose of such a memo is to inform readers of the possible consequences of the situation and either request action or commend actions taken. You do not need to go into a detailed chronological description of what happened. The main point is to discuss the implications of the situation and how best to handle the matter. The following memo to senior management illustrates this type of structure:

> As a result of the recent earthquake in Los Angeles county, our L.A. warehouse sustained considerable damage. Thus, shipment of our stuffed toys to East Coast dealers will be delayed by at least two weeks. Three dealers have reconfirmed their orders and agreed to a new delivery date, which we anticipate will be March 7. The other four dealers have not negotiated a new agreement with us. I recommend that you set up a meeting with them and offer group terms.
>
> The workers here have done a superb job pitching in to get the warehouse in order. We are at 70 percent capacity only four days after the earthquake. They all deserve commendation.

Functional Format

This organizational approach is most often used in response to a request for information. In your memo you discuss the functions of a product or person. For example, your boss may ask you to explain the difference between one copier and another. Or you may be asked to draw up job specifications for a position or to describe the duties for a part-time worker.

As in any memo, however, you would rank the information in the inverted pyramid order of importance. For example, you would describe the differences in copier quality and speed, reliability, and versatility before talking about copier size, weight, and color. In the case of job descriptions, you would list the most important duties first and less important responsibilities last.

Chronological Format

The chronological structure describes the order of events as they took place. You can either start at the beginning and move forward in time to the end, or you can state the end result and move backward in time to show how the situation developed. This format is the best choice when you must make a detailed report on the exact order of events in the workplace or on an assignment. For example:

> On October 4, at 3:36 a.m., our security guard at the West Janeway office building found that someone had circumvented the alarm system and forced their way into the building. The guard reported the break-in to the police and began a sweep of the offices. At 3:45 a.m. he discovered that three electronic typewriters, four adding machines, and our XT computer were missing from the back offices near the loading dock. The police arrived at 3:49 a.m. and made out a complete report.
>
> When I arrived for work at 8:00 a.m. that morning, I was given a copy of the police report. I telephoned our insurance agent, and he informed me that our claim should be processed within ten days. I am in the process of contacting several security companies to acquire a more sophisticated alarm system. I should be able to make a recommendation on a new system by next week. Losing the computer has been a major inconvenience for the office. We must make sure such a theft never happens again.

Question-and-Answer Format

The question-and-answer format is particularly useful when you must persuade your readers to accept or agree to something. In this sequence, you anticipate the questions your readers might ask and proceed to answer them. Your purpose is to inform the readers about desired changes or actions and to persuade them to adopt the plan you outline. In the example that follows, the sender anticipates questions employees may have about a new company parking sticker. The questions are in parentheses but would not appear in the memo.

> Nonemployee use of our company parking lot has become quite a problem in the past few months. To resolve the situation, we are issuing company parking stickers to all employees. Cars in the lot that do not display the sticker will be towed.

(Will the stickers cost anything? What time period do they cover?)

The stickers are free to all full-time employees and are good for one full year from the date they are issued. Part-time workers will pay a $10 annual fee. One-day stickers will be issued to visitors at the parking lot entrance. There is no charge for these stickers.

(Are there different stickers for visitors, management, and staff?)

The stickers are color-coded: blue for management, orange for staff and support workers, red for part-time workers, and green for visitors. Please make sure you are issued the correct sticker.

(How do we get the stickers and where on the car should they be displayed? What if we lose our stickers?)

You will receive your parking stickers from your supervisor by June 1. Display the stickers on the back of your rearview mirror so that the security team can see them easily. If you lose your sticker, request a replacement immediately. Temporary parking stickers can be obtained from the parking security guards.

This program should eliminate the frustration all of us have experienced when noncompany cars take up our parking spaces. We appreciate your cooperation in this matter.

Reporting Format

This sequence can be used to report routine information, such as sales figures or production levels, or to make simple announcements. Although you may wish to include some interpretation of the data you present, your purpose is not to persuade or convince readers to agree to something. You are simply presenting information.

When using this format, you can organize data according to various sequences; for example, by geographic regions, from highest figures to lowest, from largest to smallest divisions, and the like. The important point is to present the data so that readers can grasp the meaning quickly and easily, as in the following memo:

Vic, here are those third-quarter circulation figures you wanted for *Moneywatch*. As you can see, our sales force has done a great job boosting circulation in the Midwest.

Northeast	2,340,980. . .	up 2.3%
Mid-Atlantic	979,632. . .	no change
Southeast	865,733. . .	up 3.4%
Midwest	3,576,421. . .	up 11.4%
Southwest	345,066. . .	no change
Pacific	1,965,824. . .	up 1.3%
Northwest	433,529. . .	no change
Total	10,507,185	

Organizing Long Memos

Memos longer than three pages generally have a more formal structure than shorter messages. The main point is still the same, however: readers should not have to wade through two pages to find the point of your message. A long memo usually has the following parts:

■ *Summary* — Placed at the beginning of the memo, the summary condenses the subject to five or ten lines. It should be a clear, simple account of the subject that helps readers decide if they should read the entire memo or only certain sections. Summaries usually contain the major findings, conclusions, or recommendations listed in the memo.

If you expect a hostile reaction to your memo, you may want to begin your summary with a statement of the problem, a brief analysis, and conclusions or recommendations. In that way you may neutralize your opposition or at least get a fair hearing.

■ *Introduction* — The introduction orients the reader by stating the memo's purpose and scope. You may add a paragraph or two of background material if the reader needs more information.

The introduction can be used to ask or answer key questions, make a thank-you statement, or give good news, such as the approval of a proposal. If you must refuse a request or reject an offer, use the introduction to establish your reasons before saying "no."

■ *Discussion*—The main discussion may be limited to a few paragraphs or run several pages. The subjects may range from policy changes to reorganization of a department to a proposal for diversifying company holdings. Long memos usually discuss topics that will require considerable outlays of company resources, time, and personnel. Their arguments need to be reasonable and supported carefully, and the facts accurately identified and presented.

Your ability to outline and organize material will be crucial to this section of the memo. You can use various headings to separate your information into sections: "Statement of the Problem," "Approach to the Problem," "Analysis," "Evaluation," "Conclusions," and "Recommendations."

■ *Closing or Concluding Remarks*—The conclusion discusses what action is required of the readers. This section reviews and underscores the main points and problems your readers should keep in mind. The closing is also a place to acknowledge assistance, ask critical questions of the readers, or request a particular action or decision.

The preparation strategies in this chapter can get you started quickly and give you most of the material to write your memo. In the next chapter, we show you strategies for writing memos that communicate your message and get results.

SUMMARY

■ The basic principle in writing under pressure is to have a variety of strategies that can help you to work through mental blocks and other writing problems.

■ To begin your memo you need to (a) state your purpose and define the response you want, (b) analyze your readers, (c) know the scope and meaning of your topic, and (d) plan and organize your memo.

■ If you have trouble stating your purpose and the response you want, you can use a technique known as dialoguing.

■ To analyze your readers, consider their personal characteristics, such as gender, age, knowledge, position, and motivation. Slant your memo to their interests and needs.

■ The purpose of your memo, the response you want, and your reader profile will help you to determine the scope and meaning of your memo. Four strategies can help you at this stage: writing a laundry list, mapping, freewriting, and dialoguing.

■ Research your topic to fill in any gaps in your knowledge or any missing figures, dates, places, and so on. Make sure names of companies and recipients are spelled correctly.

■ Decide who should get copies of your message by asking who has an interest, connection, or question regarding the subject; who may need to be added or dropped from the list; and whether blind copies should be sent to your boss or anyone else.

■ Once you have established your purpose, response, reader profile, and scope of your topic, you can use several formulas to plan and organize your memo.

■ These formulas generally use the inverted pyramid sequence, which moves from the general to the specific. The exceptions are memos that are refusals, requests the reader may not want to grant, or historical background leading up to a current situation. These memos use a diamond-shaped sequence.

■ Formulas used to plan and organize memos include problem-solving, cause-and-effect, functional, chronological, question-and-answer, and reporting formats.

■ Long memos are organized into the following sections: summary, introduction, discussion, and closing or concluding remarks.

WRITING

MEMOS THAT GET ATTENTION

▼

It's 4:50 P.M. and you are about to leave the office. Two memos arrive on your desk—both on important subjects. Which one are you likely to read and which one postpone until later?

To: Your Name
From: Rhonda Stewart
Date: July 16, 19—
Subject: NEW CLIENT PROSPECT

A former client in Minneapolis gave me the name of a good prospect, Sucal Industries, that he feels we should contact immediately. The company manufactures small electrical appliances and some robotic items that look promising. For exhibits, Sucal uses display tables, stand-up signs, screens, audiovisuals, and promotional giveaways. It looks like Sucal's display packaging needs fit our product offerings perfectly.

Sucal is planning to exhibit at a major housewares and electronics expo in October. If we contact them now, we will have three months to put together a complete display package for them. This prospect sounds hot. Why don't you follow up on it? The contact at Sucal is Harrison Nunn, Director of Marketing, (213) 342-9726. We could probably get a lot of repeat business from this firm.

To: Your Name
From: Donna Marks
Date: July 16, 19—
Subject: RAYMOND INDUSTRIES PROPOSAL

A retired executive whose company has done considerable business with Raymond passed along some valuable tips for our proposal. I think they'll give us an edge over the competition.

■ Emphasize employee training in the new data processing systems. Mr. Raymond is a firm believer in thorough, on-the-job training.

■ Offer a six-month to one-year follow-up program. Raymond Industries favors companies with strong customer service features.

■ Spell out all costs in detail. Mr. Raymond has a finance background and can spot fluff quickly. Make sure all costs are fully itemized and reasonable.

Our closest competitor, Copland Systems, is weak in follow-up programs. If we can put together a solid training and follow-up package, I think we can win this job.

Any questions, give me a call at ext. 5488.

If you're like most readers, the second memo will get your attention first. Key information stands out clearly, making the message easy to read and understand. In the first memo, key information is hard to pick out from the text around it.

What makes a good memo? Why do some memos grab your attention and others irritate, frustrate, or bore you? How can your memos catch the reader's attention?

In this chapter, we take a look at how to create clear, forceful memos that get the results you want. The first section reviews memo format and outlines the structure for memo reports. The second section shows you how to build your memo from opening to closing, using two writing strategies. The last section gives tips on how to bring your words to life and hold the readers' interest from beginning to end.

MEMO FORMAT

The elements of a memo are divided into three categories: introductory lines, closing lines, and optional lines for references and attachments. These lines ensure that anyone looking at the memo will know who sent it, who the principal recipient is, the date the memo was written, its subject matter, who wrote and typed the memo, who receives copies, and what attachments or references accompany the memo.

Page formats for memos vary from company to company, as shown in Exhibit 4–1. As you can see, in some formats the introductory lines

Exhibit 4–1. Page Formats for Memos

		7882 (5-82)
INTER-OFFICE MEMO		

	NAME AND OFFICE, DIVISION OR DEPARTMENT	DATE	
TO			1
FROM	NAME AND ORIGINATING OFFICE, DIVISION OR DEPARTMENT	SUBJECT	
	MESSAGE		

213-010

ℰℬ ENCYCLOPÆDIA BRITANNICA
INTEROFFICE CORRESPONDENCE

TO _____ OFFICE _____ DATE _____

FROM _____ OFFICE _____

MEMORANDUM

are all on the left-hand side; in others, the introductory lines are placed on either side of the page. No matter how companies arrange their formats, however, they present the information in the same order.

Introductory Lines

Each memo has six headings at the top of the first page:

1. Company name and address, usually contained in the letterhead.

2. The word *Memo* or *Memorandum* centered under the letterhead. This line distinguishes the correspondence from other types of messages.

3. The word *To* followed by a colon and the name of the person or group receiving the memo. Use the reader's full name and any professional title, such as "Manager, Sales." However, you don't need to use the complimentary titles of Mr., Miss, Mrs., or Ms. For example:

> To: All part-time employees

> To: Benjamin Parsi, Vice President

If you are sending the memo to several people, you can use one of three methods, depending on the number of people in your list.

■ List the names after the word *To* in alphabetical order, unless one person clearly outranks the others. In that case, the higher ranking recipient's name comes first:

> To: Georgia Banks
>   Horace Greenway
>   Arthur Himenez

> To: Arthur Himenez, Director
>   Georgia Banks
>   Horace Greenway

■ Put only the main recipient's name at the top and list the other names at the end of the memo:

> To: Julie Trevenian, Editor in Chief

(end of memo)
cc: Carl Audoin
    Susanne Fischer
    Leslie Gervais
    Lui Jade
    Yvonne Sanchez

■ Type the line "see distribution list on page 6" after the word *To*. The list of those who receive the memo would be typed on the last page. For example:

To: See distribution list on page 6

(end of memo)
Sent to: (list of names)

4. The word *From* followed by a colon and the sender's name and professional title.

5. The word *Date* followed by a colon and the month, day, and year. All memos must be dated. This gives sender and receiver a record of their correspondence.

6. The word *Subject* followed by a colon and a line indicating the topic of the memo. The subject line should be as concise and specific as possible to catch your readers' interest.

For example, a subject line that reads "Medical Benefits" does not tell the reader much about the topic. Are benefits increasing, shrinking, becoming more expensive? Subject lines, such as "Changes in Medical Benefits" or "Increase in Medical Insurance Coverage" or "Additions to Medical Benefits" give readers a preview of the message and pique their curiosity.

Subject lines can be typed either in all capitals or with initial capitals and underscored:

Subject: CHANGES IN MEDICAL BENEFITS

Subject: Changes in Medical Benefits

Closing Lines

Memos usually have two closing lines: an initials line (for the sender and the sender's secretary or assistant) and a copies line.

1. Unlike business letters, memos are not signed by the sender. Instead, the initials (in capitals) of the writer followed by a colon and the initials (small letters) of the person who typed or prepared the memo appear two spaces below the last line of the memo.

SR:tsk

2. The abbreviation "cc" means "carbon copy." It comes from the days when carbon paper was the only way to make copies of correspondence. The abbreviation is still used to indicate who besides the primary recipients will receive the memo.

The "cc" line appears two spaces below the sender's initials. The names in the cc list do not have to be in alphabetical order, but generally the higher ranking individual is placed first.

SR:tsk

cc: Paul Sherman, Director
   Diane Chu
   Ilene Kiriakis
   Adam Beauman

The abbreviation "bcc" means "blind carbon copies." This line is used when the sender does not wish the recipient to know that copies of the memo are being sent to others. The line is typed only on the sender's copy, which is kept in the files.

SR:tsk

bcc: Calley North, Personnel Director

Optional Lines

Optional lines include references to other documents and a list of attachments. You can place these lines either at the top of the memo before the subject line or at the end of the memo following the initials or copies line.

1. *Reference lines* refer the reader to other memos, letters, reports, contracts, invoices, and the like. These documents are either the subject of the memo or supply background information the reader needs. For example:

To: Alvin Koria, Product Manager
From: Wallace Fuller, Corporate Secretary
Date: June 14, 1991
Reference: Contract #315
           Josephson & Associate, Inc.
           718 Riverside Drive
           New York, NY 10014
Subject: FINAL AMENDMENTS TO JOSEPHSON CONTRACT

If the reader needs to review reference documents, make sure you supply all information necessary to retrieve the material: file or document numbers, author's names, dates, addresses and phone numbers.

2. *Attachment lines* list photographs, diagrams, charts, correspondence, or other material attached to your memos. This line also comes before the subject line.

To: Patrice Kennedy, Art Director

From: Fredrick Ungersol, Public Relations

Date: April 6, 1991

Attachments: Color photos (3) of officers

Paper sample

Corrected brochure copy

Subject: CORPORATE PUBLIC RELATIONS BROCHURE

WRITING YOUR MEMO

Once you have done your preparation work, you are ready for the next step—writing the memo. Keep in mind the four questions that your message should answer. In your preparation work, you have determined your purpose, the characteristics of your readers, the scope of your topic, and what response you want from your readers. Now your concern is how to express yourself clearly, effectively, and concisely.

Three writing strategies can help you to accomplish this goal: (a) using shorter, more varied sentences to express your ideas; (b) using brief paragraphs, headings, lists, and emphasis devices to structure your memo; and (c) using tone, vigorous verbs, and concise wording to add power to your writing.

Most memos consist of opening sentences or paragraphs, the middle or body, and closing sentences and paragraphs. Shorter memos, such as announcements, may consist only of opening and closing sections. The writing strategies mentioned earlier will enable you to create memos that get attention no matter which organizing format you choose: problem—solution, cause-and-effect, chronological, functional, question-and-answer, or reporting sequences.

Creating the Memo: The Opening

Opening sentences or paragraphs establish the purpose of your memo. We can use Geri's memo on PAYWRITE to illustrate how you create your message. These techniques hold true for short as well as longer memos. In the preparation stage, she developed a listing of topics, slanting them toward her boss's interest in problem solving:

MEMO ON PAYWRITE

1. Accounting problems solved

    a. Earnings reports, year-end statements

    b. Debt calculations — especially foreign debt

    c. Breakdown and analysis of sales by region for all branch offices

    d. Rated highly by Arthur D. Anderson, INFOWORLD, PC WORLD, used by several major corporations

2. Productivity

    a. Boosts worker productivity — faster operations, uses less memory, more efficient use of computer networks

    b. Overall makes computers more powerful

3. Other features

    a. Better graphics

    b. Handles more variables

    c. Better compatibility with other systems in branch offices

4. Training requirements

    a. Tutorial included in software but not enough

    b. Software company will supply trainer for staff

    c. One- to two-day seminar required

5. Cost considerations

    a. Mid price range — cheaper through mail order but no service backup and no free updates

    b. Cheaper in long run — will pay for itself in time saved and increased productivity

6. Closing

    a. Recommend purchasing PAYWRITE

    b. Recommend training seminar for staff

Once you have your listing, you can use the freewriting technique to begin. For example:

> Accounting department experiencing delays and problems in producing quarterly earnings reports, year-end financial statements, sales figures for branch offices. Big part of the problem the software we are using—PAYWRITE solves these problems by giving us a superior program to generate earnings reports, year-end statements, debt calculations, and branch sales analyses. We can keep on top of our operations and spot problem areas much faster . . . gives us an advantage in fast-changing markets. Arthur D. Anderson, Inc., top accounting company gave it the highest rating and so did INFOWORLD and PC WORLD and its used by several major corporations including Bendrix and Wade Enterprises.

The question now becomes how do you turn your freewriting into concise, well-written opening sentences and paragraphs? We turn to the following writing strategy for help.

 ## WRITING STRATEGY 6: USE SHORTER, MORE VARIED SENTENCES

Sentences in business writing, like those in conversation, should average 17 to 20 words in length. Most people speak in concise sentences, but when they put their thoughts in writing, the length nearly doubles. Modern language experts find that people read and understand information better if it is packaged in smaller bites. This is not to say that all of your sentences should be short or choppy. Instead, within the 17- to 20-word limit, vary your sentence length and structure.

This strategy is easier to follow than you may think. A few guidelines can help you to break up your sentences into more digestible bits or to combine sentences.

Include only one to two ideas in each sentence. When a sentence contains more than one or two ideas, the writer appears to be free associating. Although this characteristic is fine for free-writing, your final draft must be more polished. For example:

> The new air express delivery service should speed up our overnight mailings and give us an advantage over the competition in serving the East Coast markets, which are starting to become more competitive as Ed Nestle reported in his memo last week.

The reader barely has time to absorb one idea before the next one crowds its way in. This sentence can be split into two or three.

> The new air express delivery service will speed up our overnight mailings. Faster service should give us an advantage over the competition in serving our East Coast markets. As Ed Nestle reported in his memo last week, these markets are becoming more competitive.

Shorter sentences give you an opportunity to state your purpose and catch the readers' interest right from the start. The reader has an easier time moving from topic to topic.

Watch for connecting and linking words to split or combine sentences. Words like *and*, *but*, *which*, *while*, *although*, and *however* often indicate a natural break between sentences. Look for them in your writing when you are dividing long sentences into shorter ones. For example:

> The National Toy Manufacturers project is going well. I've made an appointment to see Grace Peters about working with us on the marketing survey, *and* Henry Iona told me yesterday he would be willing to pay for part of the research.

Revised:

> The National Toy Manufacturers project is going well. I've made an appointment to see Grace Peters about working with us on the marketing survey. Yesterday, Henry Iona told me he would be willing to pay for part of the research.

Separating these sentences not only makes them easier to read but separates two ideas that are not that closely related. Again, the reader benefits from the changes.

What if you tend to write short, clipped sentences? Either use connective words, such as *however, consequently, but, although, because,* to combine some of the sentences or rewrite two sentences into one. For example:

> We can run our shoe sale ads one more week. After that we'd better shift to accessories. Valerie has a great ad layout. She still needs better written copy, though.

> **Revised:**

> We can run our shoe sale ads one more week *before shifting to the accessories sale.* Valerie has a great ad layout, *although* she still needs better copy for it.

Vary sentence construction. In speaking, we pause between ideas, our voice rises and falls for emphasis, we repeat key words or phrases, and we use facial expressions and body language to add extra meaning to our words. By comparison, the written word can appear flat and unemotional.

You can add color to your writing, however, by simply varying sentence construction. This technique mimics the rhythms and tone of natural speech and introduces a warmer, conversational mood to your messages. When sentences are all the same type, the message appears emotionally cold and monotonous, as in this memo opening.

> We attended the housewares show in Rockford on May 12 and 13. Over 120 dealers displayed their products and gave demonstrations. We talked with two kitchenware dealers interested in our packaging ideas. I will follow up these leads when I return to the office on Monday.

Revised:

On May 12 and 13 we attended the housewares show in Rockford. Over 120 dealers displayed their products and gave demonstrations. We talked with two kitchenware dealers who seemed interested in our packaging ideas. *When I return to the office on Monday*, I'll follow up these leads.

Notice how ideas flow more smoothly in the revised version. The sentences mimic the rhythms of natural speech.

Often you can vary sentence structure by turning around phrases or clauses within a sentence. For example:

> I will contact Howard Young *while I'm in New York.*
>
> *While I'm in New York,* I will contact Howard Young.

You can also vary structure by rephrasing a sentence or breaking it into two sentences.

> I'll be in New York on Thursday and will contact Howard Young.
>
> My trip will take me to New York on Thursday. In the afternoon, I should have time to contact Howard Young.

We can apply this writing strategy to Geri's memo opening. The revised freewriting would look like the following:

> The current software used by the accounting department has proven inadequate for our company's needs. Department personnel often have trouble producing on-time quarterly and year-end financial statements and sales analyses for branch offices.

After researching various accounting software, I found a program called PAYWRITE that will solve our major accounting problems. PAYWRITE offers a superior program to generate timely quarterly earnings reports, year-end statements, debt calculations, and branch office sales analyses.

With such data at our fingertips, we can monitor our operations more easily and spot problem areas faster. PAYWRITE will give us the ability to respond to rapidly changing market conditions. The program has received the highest ratings from Arthur D. Anderson, Inc., and two computer magazines, *Infoworld* and *PC World*.

Look over the memos you have written or received and do a quick word count of the sentences. Don't be surprised if they generally exceed 20 words or fall under 12. If so, use the guidelines in this section to shorten, combine, and vary your sentences for your next memo.

Creating Your Memo: The Body

The next step in creating your memo is to develop the body of your message. This means grouping ideas into paragraphs that lead the reader from one point or fact to another until you reach the closing paragraph. But large blocks of text, even when sentences are short, slow down the reader and bury your points in a welter of words.

You can use brief paragraphs, headings, and lists to create white space in your memos and break up blocks of text into more digestible bites. You can also use emphasis devices, such as capitalization, under-lining, and punctuation (dashes, parentheses, and colons), to highlight information and open up your sentences.

These techniques—like shorter, more varied sentences—help you to organize and express your thoughts. They also make it easier for your audience to read and understand your message.

WRITING STRATEGY 7: USE WHITE SPACE AND EMPHASIS DEVICES

A deft use of white space and emphasis devices highlights the main points of your message and their supporting points. The techniques appropriate for memos include:

- Brief paragraphs
- Headings
- Listings
- Capitalization, underscoring, punctuation

Brief Paragraphs

Your skill at writing short sentences will help you to create concise paragraphs as well. But how long should a paragraph be? How many points should it contain? Although no hard and fast rules exist, some guidelines can help.

To determine where paragraph breaks should occur, notice how sentences group around your ideas. Generally you mention a topic, discuss it in a few sentences, then go on to the next topic. Sentences will fall into a natural grouping around these ideas. For example:

I think the criteria the search committee has developed for selecting the new director are excellent. In particular, I like the emphasis on the candidate's possessing a finance background. However, I question the need for "experience in operations research." I think the committee is going overboard on that one. Jason Dahlworthy also asked me to draw up a list of items we need to equip the new data processing room in the finance department. See the list attached to this memo. Pam Quincy, the sales agent at Wang, indicated we could get a sizable discount on electronic equipment. Let's talk about this next week.

The sentences in this paragraph naturally group around two topics: the search committee's criteria and the new equipment. You would break the text into two shorter paragraphs.

I think the criteria the search committee has developed for selecting the new director are excellent. In particular, I like the emphasis on the candidate's possessing a finance background. However, I question the need for "experience in operations research." I think the committee is going overboard on that one.

Jason Dahlworthy also asked me to draw up a list of items we need to equip the new data processing room in the finance department. See the list attached to this memo. Pam Quincy, the sales agent at Wang, indicated we could get a sizable discount on electronic equipment. Let's talk about this next week.

Discuss only one idea in a paragraph. As shown in the earlier example, sentences group around a single topic. Make sure that each paragraph develops only one idea. In general, paragraphs that run over five or six sentences probably contain too many topics and should be split.

Use key sentences — called topic sentences — to introduce or summarize your paragraph topic. Remember the purpose of a paragraph is to discuss one idea, present a brief explanation or example, and stop. The opening paragraph in Geri's memo places the topic sentence first.

The current software used by the account department has proved inadequate for our company's needs. Department personnel often have trouble producing on-time quarterly and year-end financial statements and sales analyses for branch offices.

Every sentence in the paragraph should discuss only the inadequacies of the department's current software. A topic sentence at the end of the paragraph would look like the following:

The accounting department has had repeated difficulty generating timely quarterly earnings reports. Also, branch offices have complained that accounting is often late with their monthly sales breakdowns and analyses. Accounting personnel maintain that the delays are caused by an inadequate software program. *To solve our accounting problems we need to replace the current software with a more powerful, versatile program.*

Headings

Headings can highlight your topics and lead the reader quickly through your message. Look over your initial list of topics to determine what your headings should be and where they should occur in the memo. When writing headings, keep these guidelines in mind:

Good headings are informative and short. Like the subject line, headings give readers a clear idea of the topic to be discussed. Suppose, for example, you are evaluating the merits of two computers. Your headings should tell the reader what you will cover in the paragraphs that follow.

Poor: IBM AND APPLE PCs (too broad a category)

Better: COMPARISON OF IBM AND APPLE PCs (tells the reader to expect a discussion of the comparative strengths and weaknesses of the two computers)

Good headings should be brief, no more than one or two lines. You want to tell the reader *something* about the topic without having to say *everything*.

Poor: HOW NEW FEDERAL GOVERNMENT IMPORT–EXPORT REGULATIONS WILL AFFECT OUR DOMESTIC AND OVERSEAS SUBSIDIARIES

Better: EFFECTS OF NEW IMPORT–EXPORT REGULATIONS ON SUBSIDIARIES

Good headings have parallel construction. Make sure your headings are written in the same style throughout your memo. If you want to begin with a verb form or noun, for example, make sure all headings begin with a verb form or a noun. If you start out with phrases, all your headings should be phrases. Don't throw in a sentence as a heading.

Poor: CURRENT CONTRACT TERMS
NEGOTIATE NEW TERMS IN THE CONTRACT
WHO SHOULD SIGN THIS CONTRACT

Better: CURRENT CONTRACT TERMS
NEW TERMS TO NEGOTIATE
AUTHORIZED SIGNERS OF THE CONTRACT

In the revised version, all the headings start with an adjective modifying a key noun. Parallel structure helps the reader grasp the flow of your message more easily.

Headings are never used as the first sentence of the paragraph that follows the heading. If your heading is FIRST-QUARTER DOMESTIC SALES, don't start out the paragraph saying, *"They are up 10 percent over the same period last year."* Instead say, *"First-quarter sales for all domestic branches ..."* or *"Domestic sales for the first quarter ..."*

Headings are never used singly—you must have at least two headings in your memo. Headings introduce a series of two or more topics. A single heading serves no purpose; you can use other methods—lists or brief paragraphs—to emphasize your topic. Your subject line serves as a heading for the entire memo.

Headings can be set either flush with the left-hand margin or indented. They are usually typed in all capitals and may be underscored.

Flush left heading:

RECOMMENDED SITE FOR NEW PLANT
After studying several sites in great detail, the committee
recommends that we purchase the San Antonio, Texas, property.

Indented heading:

RECOMMENDED SITE FOR NEW PLANT
After studying several sites in great detail, the committee
recommends that we purchase the San Antonio, Texas,
property.

Geri's memo is a good example of how headings can enhance a message. She can use her numbered topics to determine what headings she needs.

PAYWRITE AND OUR ACCOUNTING PROBLEMS
Discussion of accounting problems solved by PAYWRITE's
accounting program.

PAYWRITE AND INCREASED PRODUCTIVITY
Discussion of how PAYWRITE increases productivity through its superior software.

ADDITIONAL FEATURES OF PAYWRITE
Discussion of other features of the program that would interest the reader.

TRAINING REQUIREMENTS FOR ACCOUNTING STAFF
Discussion of what training is needed, how it would be arranged, and how much it would cost.

COST CONSIDERATIONS
Discussion of cost of PAYWRITE and how the cost would be justified by the program's superior features.

RECOMMENDATIONS
Recommendation to purchase the program and conduct training for staff.

Good headings can be used even in one-page memos if they will help the reader understand the message more easily. For example, an insurance manager wrote the following memo to her boss, using a problem–solution format:

To: Richard Hardesty, Regional Vice President
From: Gail Fraser, Manager Customer Affairs
Date: October 7, 19—
Reference: Term Life Insurance Policy 1499720
Subject: ACCIDENTAL LAPSE OF CUSTOMER POLICY

Last week I discovered that one of our office staff had accidentally allowed a customer's term life insurance policy to lapse. This customer purchased the term life policy under our option to convert to whole term life insurance within three months.

PROBLEM

Under our current regulations, the customer must reapply for a whole term policy and submit to a physical exam again. However, the policy lapse was our error, not the customer's fault.

REMEDY

I recommend that we waive the requirements for reapplication and the physical exam in this customer's case. Because Mutual made the mistake, I believe we should bear the consequences. We can reinstate the customer's term policy and convert to whole life as if no interruption in service had occurred.

Please let me know your decision on this matter as soon as possible.

Lists

Bulleted, numbered, or lettered lists also make your memo more inviting to read and draw attention to your main points. Compare the two versions that follow:

We have set three company goals for the 1992-93 fiscal year. We want to establish ourselves as a maker of quality educational toys, expand our product line to include computer learning games, and gain a greater share of the elementary-high school educational market.

Revised:

We have set three company goals for the 1992-93 fiscal year:

- Establish ourselves as a maker of quality educational toys.
- Expand our product line to include computer learning games.
- Gain a greater share of the elementary-high school educational market.

The first version obscures the three goals in a solid block of text. The revised version emphasizes them, enabling the reader to grasp the three goals more easily.

To make the best use of the listing technique, follow these guidelines:

- *Use bullets or small letter "o's" for lists when the order of the points is not important.*

■ *Use numbers or letters when you need to prioritize items in your lists (e.g., procedures, objectives, instructions).*

■ *Write your lists in parallel form.* Make sure they begin with the same part of speech (verb form, adjective, noun); are roughly the same length; and have the same structure (all phrases, all sentences, all questions, etc.).

When all items in a list begin in different ways, readers have a harder time understanding and following your points. Look over the example below.

Poor:

Please follow these four steps when using the copying machine:

1. After lifting the cover, place the original face down on the glass and close the cover again.

2. You must select the number of copies you want, the size paper, and adjust the toner.

3. Close the cover and press the START button, waiting until the READY light flashes before lifting the cover and removing your original.

4. Removing your original, close the cover when you are through.

Better:

Please follow these four steps when using the copying machine:

1. Lift the cover and place the original face down on the glass, then close the cover.

2. Select number of copies, the correct paper size, and tone setting.

3. Press the START button. Wait until the READY light flashes before lifting the cover again.

4. Remove your original and close the cover when finished copying.

The revised version uses verb forms to begin all four points (lift, select, press, remove), leading the reader quickly from one step to the next.

■ *In general, limit your lists to three to five points.* A long list or series of lists will have the same numbing effect on the reader as a solid block of text. The idea is to make your points stand out, not convert all your sentences into lists.

Capitalization, Underscoring, Punctuation

You can also highlight information or create white space in your memos by a selective use of capitalization, underscoring, and punctuation (dashes, parentheses, and colons). In Geri's memo, for example, the name of the software, PAYWRITE, is written in all capitals to set it off from the surrounding text.

The key word in this technique is *selective* use. Too much underlining or capitalization, for example, dilutes the effect you want to make on the reader.

Poor:

Please note the following regulations for *shipping overseas packages.*

   1. All packages must be properly sealed with GUMMED TAPE, PACKING TAPE, OR FIBERGLASS TAPE.

   2. Include *name, address, and shipping number* on the label.

   3. All packages *must carry enough postage for RETURN. There will be no exceptions*—in the past merchandise was lost because shippers did not want to pay for return postage.

   4. Mail room must be notified AT LEAST *two days* in advance of any large mailings.

PLEASE FOLLOW THESE REGULATIONS CAREFULLY.

Better:

The following regulations apply to all overseas packages.

   1. Seal all packages with *gummed, packing, or fiberglass tape.*

   2. Include name, address, and shipping number on the label.

3. Make sure you have included RETURN POSTAGE. We don't want to lose merchandise because the customer has to pay for returns.

4. Notify the mail room at least *two days* in advance if you have a large mailing.

We ask your cooperation in following these regulations carefully.

Consider the element of tact when using capitalization and underlining. You want to avoid the impression that you are shouting at the reader or implying that the reader is too dumb to catch the main points without considerable help from you.

The use of punctuation can open your sentences and highlight information. Again, use these devices sparingly. Dashes, for example, set off ideas or topics within a sentence.

Computer companies—even industry leaders like Utica—predict slower sales next year.

Parentheses also call attention to ideas or refer the reader to other data but in a more subtle way. The parenthetical break should be as brief and nonintrusive as possible.

Poor:

Mutual funds represent a sound investment for many nonprofit companies (see attached copy of *Forbes* article in which mutual funds are rated among the top ten high-yield investments of the past five years).

Better:

Mutual funds represent a sound investment for many nonprofit companies (see attached copy of *Forbes* article).

Colons set off information within a sentence. Like dashes, they break up text visually and can highlight an idea or series within a paragraph.

Hydigger Farms specializes in growing wheat and alfalfa. These crops respond particularly well to three of our fertilizers: Compound 4D, Hi-Yield, and Alfagrow T6.

Make sure you have a good reason for using punctuation devices to break up your sentences. Don't overdo their use or throw them in arbitrarily. Like everything else in your memo, their presence should strengthen and clarify your message.

The skillful use of brief paragraphs, headings, lists, and emphasis devices can greatly enhance your writing. They make your memo more visually appealing and increase its impact on the reader.

Creating Your Memo: The Closing

In many cases, the closing sentence or paragraph in your memo lets your reader know what response you want. Do you need a decision, recommendation, opinion, action, compliance, agreement, change in behavior?

The closing can be a simple sentence, "Let me know when we can discuss the diet drink campaign," or a paragraph outlining information you need. Make sure your readers clearly understand why you are communicating with them.

The nature of your closing will depend on your purpose for writing the memo. Suppose you are writing a memo to correct or reprimand someone for recent, chronic tardiness. If it is a first warning, you might close with the following:

> Your fine record in the past indicates you are a conscientious employee and take pride in your work. I'm sure you will make every effort to report for work on time.

Your final paragraph states what you want the person to do and affirms your confidence in his/her ability to comply. If the reprimand is a second or third warning, however, your closing statement is likely to be stronger.

> You have been warned previously about arriving late for work. If you are tardy again, we will be forced to place you on three months' probation. You will not receive another warning.

TIPS FOR LIVELY WRITING

Now that you have organized your memo and made it visually appealing to the reader, you need to focus on your language. *How you say something* can be as important as *what you have to say.* The writing strategy that follows shows you how to add power and energy to your writing.

If you want your message to have an impact on the reader, pay careful attention to your tone, the verbs you use, and the concise wording of your ideas.

▶ ## WRITING STRATEGY 8: TONE, VIGOROUS VERBS, AND CONCISE WORDING

Tone and the Writer's Attitude

Tone refers to the emotional content of your memos, the level of formality or informality you adopt in communicating, and your attitude toward your topic. Tone lets your readers know that you are communicating specifically with *them* and not with just anyone.

Create "reader-based" messages. Whenever possible, maintain a personal touch and emphasize *you* over *me* in your memos. Instead of writing to your workers "I want to emphasize the importance of following safety procedures," why not say "Your safety is important to this company. Please follow all safety procedures carefully to avoid accidents."

Emphasize the positive. In general, you want to keep your tone positive and upbeat and to avoid negativity, sarcasm, or inappropriate humor. Even when writing a reprimand or pointing out a problem, your tone should be firm but evenhanded. Remember your purpose is to change behavior or to find a solution, not to browbeat, offend, or degrade another. Compare the two examples that follow:

Inappropriate tone:

Bill, obviously somebody in your office can't read. This is the second time this month I've had to return the overtime records because the client job numbers weren't filled in. Give the job to somebody else this time, okay? Or at least tell them the facts—no overtime records, no overtime pay.

Appropriate tone:

Bill, I'm returning your overtime records because the client job numbers were not filled in. This oversight has occurred twice in one month.

Please let your staff know that unless we have complete records, we can't issue overtime checks. I appreciate your help in clearing up this problem.

If you find yourself in a negative mood when you sit down to write, try to change your attitude. Take a walk, make a phone call, do something to burn off some of that negative energy. Or write a negative memo *but don't send it*. Firing off a broadside at someone may make you feel good, but think how it would feel to be on the receiving end of it. Short-term satisfaction is a poor trade-off for creating long-term problems for yourself.

Keep the tone conversational. With the exception of highly technical messages, memos by their very nature are informal communications. Yet many writers feel that when they put their thoughts on paper, they must change their language into something more official sounding. The result is usually stuffy or stilted:

Herewith are the files for the Andover audit. Please make an estimate of your requirements for the length of time you will need these files. Note this time on the enclosed slip and return the slip to me at your earliest convenience.

This writer obviously believes that a more official tone is likely to ensure the reader's compliance. It's more likely to ensure the reader's confusion. The writer needed only to say:

Here are the files for the Andover audit. Please let me know how long you will need them. Write your time estimate on the attached slip and return the slip to me.

Stuffy language clogs up communication and obscures meaning. *Hear* yourself telling the reader what you want him or her to know before you write it. Read your message aloud. Strive for a clear, straightforward style that lets your true "voice" come through.

Avoid mixing tones in a message. Make sure that your tone is appropriate for your reader's position. You would use a more formal tone with superiors and a more relaxed, informal tone with colleagues or subordinates. A memo to someone above you in the organization should not be too familiar or assume too much about your relationship. In general, avoid mixing tones, as in the example below:

Inappropriate tone:

To: Cornelia Holmes, Vice President
From: Opal Harris, Assistant Manager
Subject: HIRING PART-TIME CLERICAL HELP

Because of the recent loss of two full-time employees, I've found myself shorthanded—and you know how hectic that can be! Last time this happened we didn't catch up for three weeks! I would like approval to hire two temporary clerical workers for the month of March. We're always busiest then—it must be the spring weather.

Please let me know as soon as possible if we can take on the extra help. By the way, I love your new hairdo.

The mixed tone and inappropriate personal comments of this memo are not likely to endear its writer to Cornelia Holmes. Ms. Harris should have focused on her request and saved the personal comments for conversation.

Appropriate tone:

To: Cornelia Holmes, Vice President
From: Opal Harris, Assistant Manager
Subject: HIRING PART-TIME CLERICAL HELP

Two clerical workers in our department resigned last week, leaving us shorthanded for the workload in March. I would like your approval to hire two temporary clerical workers to cover that month. Because you will be out of town next week, I would be willing to make all arrangements to hire and train the part-time workers.

Please let me know as soon as possible if we can take on the extra help.

The revised memo not only states a problem and what decision is needed but lets the vice president know what the manager is willing to do to help. The tone is businesslike without being too familiar or too stuffy.

Increase your business writing skills by learning to use various tones for different readers and situations.

Vigorous Verbs

Verbs add energy and power to your writing. Weak verbs can dilute the effectiveness of your entire message. To improve your writing, keep these two guidelines in mind:

1. Use action verbs, not state-of-being verbs.
2. Use the active voice, not the passive voice.

Action verbs. Action verbs show the reader that something is happening or that someone is taking action. These verbs move your sentences along and engage the reader. Avoid overusing *can* or *should* and all forms of the verb *to be—am, is, are, was, were, will be, been, being.* These static verbs forms are like a still photograph compared to a live action film.

Whenever possible, change a state-of-being verb into an action verb. For example:

> The new furnace plans *are in violation* of
> several OSHA regulations.

The verb *are* simply sits in the middle of the sentence. The strongest word is *violation.* By changing it to a verb, you strengthen the entire sentence and catch the reader's attention.

> The new furnace plans *violate* several
> OSHA regulations.

Frequently, verbs are buried in nouns that end in "ion" or "tion," such as *authorization, application, completion, production*. These nouns can be changed into verbs, saving your sentences from excessive "noun-ism." For instance, changing "my supervisor gave authorization" to "my supervisor authorized" creates a stronger impression.

Other verbs, such as *to do, to seem, to appear,* or *to make,* lack power as well. See if you can choose other verbs that work harder for you. Compare the two sentences that follow:

> Weak: The instructions *are* applicable to all personnel who *do* their work on word processors.

> Better: The instructions *apply* to all personnel who *work* on word processors.

Such simple changes tighten up your sentences and enhance their impact on the reader.

Active over passive voice. The active voice, like active verbs, adds interest and liveliness to your writing. It describes who or what carried out an action.

> I *sent* the letter. Congress *passed* the bill. The explosion *damaged* our South Holland plant.

The passive voice is more static and describes who or what received the action.

> The letter *was sent* by me. The bill *was passed* by Congress. Our South Holland plant *was damaged* by the explosion.

Besides adding unnecessary words to your sentences, the passive voice obscures the actors in your message. Compare the two memos that follow:

> I understand that the Tri-Arts loan is three months delinquent. Repeated past-due notices *have been sent* to Tri-Arts but none of them *has been answered*. This loan *was granted* on April 20,

1988, on the condition that all payments *were to be made* by
the fifteenth (15th) of each month.

Who *granted, sent, didn't answer, made payments*? Shifting to the
active voice brings the actors back into the picture and lends more
force to the memo.

I understand that Tri-Arts Production is three months delinquent on
their loan payments. Our billing manager *has sent* repeated past-
due notices to Tri-Arts management, but they *have not responded*.
We *granted* Tri-Arts this loan on April 20, 1988, on the condition
that they *would make* all payments by the fifteenth (15th) of each
month.

In general, change the passive voice to the active voice whenever you can.

Diplomatic passive voice. The only time the passive voice may
be preferred over the active voice is in sensitive situations. Perhaps
you don't want the actor known or you want to shift the focus from
who did something to *what* can be done about it. For example:

On Tuesday a customer's order *was delivered* to the wrong
location. Through the quick thinking of the delivery department,
we located another shipment and filled the order on time. I'd like
to thank Greg Long and his crew for their timely action. (No one
needs to know that a new employee—nervous on his first job—
made the mistake.)

Use the diplomatic passive voice sparingly, however. For
most memos, the active voice serves you better.

Eliminating Excess Words and Phrases

Concise writing means eliminating unnecessary words that interfere
with clear communication. To help you cut out empty phrases,
clichés, and buzz words from your writing, imagine that each word
in your memo costs you money. The more unnecessary words you

cut, the more money you save. With enough practice, you will automatically eliminate these words and phrases as you draft your message.

Unnecessary introductory or qualifying words and phrases simply clutter up your sentences. Eliminate them from your writing, using the following guidelines:

Avoid the phrases "there is," "there are," "there was," "there were." These words weaken your sentences. Omit them and instead put the most important information up front. Rewrite the sentences using more active verbs.

> Poor : *There are* four suppliers competing for Drexler's business.

> Better : Four suppliers *are competing* for Drexler's bussiness.

> Poor : As Tricia Dowling mentioned, *there is* a Far Eastern market that's opened up for our products.

> Better : As Tricia Dowling mentioned, a Far Eastern market *has opened up* for our products.

Condense clauses beginning with "which," "that," *or* "who" *into fewer words.* These qualifying clauses can be trimmed to a few words, conveying your message more emphatically.

> Poor : The director *who came from the East Coast* suggested *that we should* increase our technical staff.

> Better : The *East Coast director suggested* we increase our technical staff.

> Poor : The decline, *which occurred last year*, has delayed new product plans *that the committee approved in July*.

> Better : *Last year's decline* has delayed the *committee's new product plans*, approved in July.

Eliminate wordy and redundant phrases from your writing. These phrases often repeat the meaning of main words or add unnecessary emphasis to words whose meaning is already clear.

> Poor : The corrugated boxes are rectangular *in shape*.
> ("Rectangular" is a shape.)

Better : The corrugated boxes are rectangular.

Poor : *During the course of* the presentation.... (During means "during the course of.")

Better : *During* the presentation....

What follows is a list of wordy phrases that commonly turn up in business writing. Change wordy phrases to their more concise alternatives wherever you find them in your own writing.

Wordy	*Concise*
in about a week's time	in about a week
blue in color	blue
speaking on a theoretical basis	speaking theoretically
consensus of opinion	consensus
in the vast majority of cases	in most cases
in spite of the fact that	although
personal in manner	personal
refer back to	refer to
engaged in a study of	studying
depreciates in value	depreciates
opening gambit	gambit
few in number	few
until such time as	until
due to the fact that	because
very necessary	necessary
in the amount of $5.00	for $5.00
between the hours of 2–5 P.M.	between 2–5 P.M.
empty vacuum	vacuum

Don't belabor the obvious. Some writers start out their sentences by explaining the obvious: "That is to say," "In other words," "To make a point," "As you may know." Why not simply start the sentence? Such phrases dilute the force of the words that follow. If you've stated something clearly, why say it again in other words? In general, avoid such phrases in your writing.

Omit clichés and buzz words. Clichés are tired, overworked phrases that say nothing of any substance. They come easily to mind when we write because they are an ingrained part of everyday language. Resist the temptation to use them; instead, find more precise language to convey your meaning.

> *Poor:* I think Harold is *off the beam* on his evaluation of Karen's project. If he tries to press his point, his argument *won't hold water.* (The clichés "off the beam" and "won't hold water" say nothing specific about Harold's argument.)
>
> *Better:* I think Harold has missed the value of Karen's project. If he tries to press his point, he'll only reveal the weaknesses in his own argument.

Clichés in a memo indicate a lazy mind. Root out these overworked phrases and keep your language vivid and fresh. Common clichés in business writing include:

last but not least

in the final analysis

keep a low profile

seeing (or not seeing) eye to eye on an issue

in actual fact

can't see the forest for the trees

Buzz words are business slang that, like clichés, add little to the meaning of your sentences. Delete them and substitute more appropriate words. Some of today's buzz words include:

Buzz words	Alternatives
marketwise (or anything -wise)	market
bottom line	main point
parameter	limit, boundary
interface	work together
feedback	opinion, response

Eliminate all words, phrases, ideas, and information that are not essential to your message. Use the appropriate tone and strong, active verbs to add energy to your writing. By following the guidelines in this strategy, you will capture the attention and earn the respect of your readers.

In the next chapter we look at the final step in creating your memo—the review process.

SUMMARY

■ Memo format consists of introductory lines, closing lines, and optional lines for references and attachments.

■ Three writing strategies can help you express your ideas clearly, effectively, and concisely: (a) use shorter, more varied sentences; (b) use brief paragraphs, headings, lists, and emphasis devices; and (c) use tone, vigorous verbs, and concise wording.

■ Most memos contain opening sentences or paragraphs, the middle or body, and closing sentences or paragraphs.

■ Opening paragraphs establish the purpose of your memo. Shorter, more varied sentences can capture the readers' attention.

■ Sentences should range from 17 to 20 words. Follow these guidelines when writing:

— Include only one to two ideas in each sentence.

— Watch for connecting and linking words to split or combine sentences.

— Vary sentence construction.

■ The body of the memo develops the main points of your message. You can use brief paragraphs, headings, lists, and emphasis devices to create white space in your memo and break up blocks of text into more digestible bites.

■ Paragraphs develop each point in your memo. Guidelines for writing good paragraphs include:

— Determine where paragraph breaks should occur.

— Notice how sentences group around your ideas.

— Discuss only one idea in a paragraph.

— Use key sentences—called topic sentences—to introduce or summarize your paragraph topic.

■ Headings highlight your topics and lead the reader quickly through your message.

- Good headings are short and informative.
- Good headings are written in parallel form.
- Headings are never used as the first sentence of the paragraph that follows.
- Headings are never used singly—you must have at least two headings in your memo.
- Headings can be set either flush with the left-hand margin or indented.

■ Bulleted, numbered, or lettered lists make your memo more inviting to read and draw attention to your main points.

- Use bullets or small letter *o*'s for lists when the order of the points is not important.
- Use numbers or letters when you need to prioritize items (e.g., procedures, objectives, instructions).
- Write your lists in parallel form.
- In general, limit your lists to three to five points.

■ Capitalization, underscoring, and punctuation (dashes, parentheses, and colons) also highlight information and create white space within paragraphs. However, they should be used selectively.

■ The closing sentence or paragraph lets your reader know what response you want. The nature of your closing will depend on your purpose for writing the memo.

■ Tone refers to the emotional content of your memos, the level of formality or informality you adopt, and your attitude toward your topic.

- Create "reader-based" messages that emphasize *you* over *me*.
- Emphasize the positive in your messages.
- Keep your tone conversational.
- Avoid mixing tones in a message.

■ Verbs add energy and power to your writing. Use action verbs, not state-of-being verbs, and use the active voice, not the passive voice. The diplomatic passive voice may be used in sensitive situations when you wish to emphasize the event and not the actor.

■ Concise writing means eliminating excess words that interfere with clear communication.

- Avoid the phrases *there is, there are, there was, there were.*
- Condense clauses beginning with *which, that,* or *who* into fewer words.
- Eliminate wordy and redundant phrases.
- Don't belabor the obvious.
- Avoid clichés and buzz words.

CHAPTER FIVE

REVIEW

GETTING THE WORDS
JUST RIGHT

▼

Geri asked Frank to review her final memo to Mr. Grant. Frank read it over, then said, "I understand everything in your memo but the last part. Who pays for staff training — our company or the software firm?"

"Don't I mention that?"

"No, all you say is 'the training will cost a maximum of $500 for the entire staff.' Not a word about who foots the bill."

"*We* do. I'd better stick in a sentence saying so."

"Also, unless I missed something, I don't think we'll be able to buy PAYWRITE for $40. Shouldn't that be $400?"

"Let me see...." Geri looked at the figure and felt her face get hot. "Yes, it should. Thanks, Frank, I owe you one."

Brian gave his finished memo to a colleague, Karla Patchen, to review. Half way through the memo she asked:

"Where's the third point?"

"The what?"

"Right here in the second paragraph you say, 'The legislation will limit us in three ways,' but you discuss only two. Did they change the bill already?"

"I *had* three points but took one out. I guess I forgot to change the second paragraph."

CARELESS ERRORS, VAGUE wording, poor organization — even one or two mistakes can lower the credibility of your entire message. Readers will wonder — if you can't get the simple things right how can we trust the rest of what you have to say?

In this chapter we discuss the final step in the writing process—review. The time you take to ensure clarity, conciseness, and accuracy is time well invested in good communication. We also include a brief section on the most troublesome grammar points for many writers and conclude with guidelines for proofreading your message.

REVIEW: THE FINAL STEP

The review process is your last chance to check your memo before sending it out with your name on it. Make sure you have answered the four key questions, crafted your language, checked your grammar and your facts, and proofread the final version for typographical mistakes and other errors.

The writing strategy in this chapter gives you a checklist for your review process.

 # WRITING STRATEGY 9: REVIEW CHECKLIST

1. Is the Format Completed Correctly?

Have you filled in all the introductory lines? Is the memo properly addressed and dated? Have all attachments or references been listed? Look at your subject line—does it tell the reader enough about the topic covered in your message or is it too broad or too narrow?

Are the closing lines completed? Have you carefully considered who should receive copies? Check to see that you have listed the recipients' names in alphabetical order or that the senior member heads the list.

2. Have I Stated My Purpose Clearly?

Look over your opening sentences or paragraphs to see if you have clearly stated the purpose of your memo. If your audience had time to read only the first few lines of the message would they know why you are writing? Don't leave them guessing. Eliminate unnecessary introductory material, wordy phrases, or background information that obscures your point.

Unclear:

To: Anton Roundtree, Vice President, Production
From: Patricia Farkas, Human Resources
Subject: CANDIDATES FOR QUALITY CONTROL MANAGER

As you know, the position of quality control manager is one of the most important in the production department. If it is left open too long, it can seriously affect our production standards. As a result, I have selected four candidates to interview for the position next week in the hope we can fill the job as soon as possible.

It's safe to assume that the production VP knows the importance of having a quality control manager. The first two sentences are unnecessary. The point of the memo should be a progress report on the interview process.

Revised:

To: Anton Roundtree, Vice President, Production
From: Patricia Farkas, Human Relations
Subject: CANDIDATES FOR QUALITY CONTROL MANAGER

I have selected four candidates from among fifteen respondents for the quality control manager's position. Two of the candidates, although less experienced, have backgrounds in robotics and product engineering. If all goes well, I should be able to choose the final candidates for you to interview by the end of this month.

The revised version lets the vice president know exactly what's going on in the selection process. If he wants to know more about the four candidates, he can contact Pat Farkas.

3. Have I Analyzed My Readers?

Is your message reader based rather than writer based? Do you know something about your readers' characteristics and what motivates them? Make sure your tone and language level are appropriate to the person you are addressing. If you use jargon, technical terms, or abbreviations, will your readers understand what you are saying?

4. Have I Determined the Scope and Meaning of My Topic?

How much do you need to say about your subject and what do your readers really need to know? As you read through your memo, ask yourself if the information you have presented is essential to the topic or merely "nice to know." Delete nonessential information that clutters up your memo and interferes with your main points.

Unclear:

> The conference featured one excellent seminar on planning, but most of the talks were pretty dull and the food was even worse. The talks dealt with issues we've already solved like transportation modeling, pricing strategies, and dealerships. One speaker even brought in a blackboard — talk about shades of business school! The planning seminar, though, gave me some great ideas to streamline our planning process the next time around.

The paragraph's most important point — the excellent seminar on planning — is lost while the writer talks about seminars irrelevant to the company. The side trip would be appropriate in conversation but not in a memo where every word counts. The reader is left asking, "What about the planning seminar?"

Revised:

> Most of the seminars at the conference covered issues we've already solved, but the session on planning was excellent. I think we can use the following points to streamline our planning process next year:
>
> ■ Appoint a marketing controller to coordinate all marketing plans.

■ Use the portfolio method to project product performance and help to select marketing strategies.

■ Develop a uniform questionnaire to analyze our competition.

The revised version spells out what the writer learned that may benefit the company. No words are wasted on unimportant topics. If readers want to find out about the other seminars — or what the food was like — they can talk to the writer.

5. Have I Stated Clearly What Response I Want from the Reader?

If you require some action or response from your readers, have you stated clearly in the closing sentences or paragraphs what you want? Don't assume that your readers will infer from your message what response to give. ("Surely they'll know I need an answer by Thursday.") Mind reading is not part of the communication process between sender and receiver. State clearly what you want.

Unclear:

Put in an order for 15 boxes of printer ribbons. By the way, I noticed Quill has a sale on 9″ × 12″ envelopes. Why don't we order some? We have a big mailing ahead of us, and we're short on this item. You can bill my department.

Ordering the envelopes on sale is a great idea — but how many? When are they needed? The reader will have to call the writer to find out. With a few moments' thought, the writer could have filled in those details.

Revised:

Put in an order for 15 boxes of printer ribbons. By the way, I noticed Quill has a sale on 9″ × 12″ envelopes. Please order 500

of them. We have a big mailing coming up, so we'll need delivery
by February 5. You can bill the item to my department.

The revised memo leaves no doubt about how many and when. It
takes only a few extra moments to answer such questions, but it
can save you and your readers a great deal of time and frustration.

6. Is My Memo Well Organized?

Good organization ensures the logical flow of ideas from one paragraph to another in the body of your memo. Look over the various
memo sequences listed in Chapter 3, beginning with the inverted
pyramid or diamond structure through the reporting sequence.

Read through your memo and circle your main point. Except
for the diamond structure, if your main point comes in the middle
or at the end of the memo, your organization is faulty. Revise your
message so that the main point appears in the opening lines or
follows immediately after the introductory material in the diamond
sequence.

Once you have established your main point, rank the following
points in your memo in order of importance. If any of these points
are out of sequence, revise your memo so that the logical flow
moves from most important to least important point. Your readers
should not encounter a key fact in the third paragraph that should
appear in the second.

7. Have I Varied My Sentence Length and Construction?

Read your memo aloud, paying particular attention to the length
and construction of your sentences. Do your sentences average 17
to 20 words or less? Have you varied their construction to mimic
the rhythms of natural speech?

Good sentence structure helps the reader move quickly and
easily through your memo. If your sentences are too short or
too long, overly complex or monotonous, they detract from your
message. Your sentences should draw attention to the *information*
they contain, not to themselves.

8. Have I Made Good Use of White Space and Emphasis Devices?

The main purpose of brief paragraphs, headings, lists, and emphasis devices is to highlight your key points and to make the memo more inviting to read. As you review your memo, make sure you have

- Discussed only one topic per paragraph.
- Kept your headings brief, informative, and parallel. Do your headings give the reader an accurate indication of the topics covered?
- Listed topics where appropriate. Would information buried in paragraphs be better set in a list? Have you limited your lists to three to five items? Are the items parallel and roughly the same length? Do you use too many lists?
- Made selective use of capitalization, underlining, and dashes, parentheses, or colons.

9. Is My Language Vivid and Concise?

Have you used active verbs and changed the passive voice to active voice? Can you eliminate *there is* and *there are* from the beginning of your sentences and start out more forcefully? Can you condense clauses beginning with *which*, *who*, and *that* into fewer words?

Reread your memo to see where you can trim wordy phrases and redundancies, and replace clichés and buzz words with your own language.

WATCH YOUR GRAMMAR

Keep a good dictionary, thesaurus, and grammar book handy for reference when you write. A good grammar reference can answer all your questions regarding punctuation, verb forms, parts of speech, abbreviations, capitalization, and other style questions. Various editing software also can be used to correct your memo.

In this chapter, we provide easy guidelines for grammar questions about punctuation, subject—verb agreement, capitalization, abbreviations, and numbers. Many business people find such questions the most troublesome when they write. In the Appendixes, we include lists of commonly confused words and frequently misspelled words.

Punctuation

Punctuation is used to show where one thought ends and another begins; to indicate relationships between ideas; to separate items in a sentence or a series; and to express measures of time, quantity, weight, and so on. The most common punctuation marks used in memos include periods, commas, semicolons, colons, dashes, parentheses, and quotation marks.

Period. The period marks a full stop at the end of a statement, command, or request. It is also used in many abbreviations. When the abbreviation comes at the end of a sentence, only one period is used.

EXAMPLES:

The director called a meeting for Monday. (statement)

Call Peterson by Friday. (command)

Please return the reply slip today. (request)

Lau said the order could be shipped F.O.B. (abbreviation)

Wetlands, Inc., approved the Dec. 5 deadline. (abbreviations)

Commas. Commas are among the most irksome of punctuation marks for writers. Yet the rules for their use are quite simple.

■ *Series* — commas are used to separate items in a series. Insert a comma before the final *and, but,* or *or* to avoid any confusion regarding the last two items in a series.

EXAMPLE:

Frank mentioned that we need to hire a payroll clerk, two administrative assistants, a sales manager, and a public relations officer.

■ *Joining two sentences* — use a comma before *and, but, or, yet, for* when they join two complete sentences, unless the sentences are very short.

EXAMPLES:

Mr. Norton may not be ready to sign the agreement tomorrow, *but* I'll have the contract ready just in case. He'll talk to Gwen, *and* she'll call you.

NOTE: Do not use a comma before *and, but, or, yet, for* when they join two verbs that share the same subject. Do not separate a subject and verb or two subordinate clauses joined by a conjunction with a comma.

He'll *talk* to Gwen *and call* you on Thursday. (The verbs *talk* and *call* share the same subject *He*.)

The IRS agent informed us *that we have limited tax liability* and *that our quarterly payments are adequate*. (The two subordinate clauses — in italics — are not separated by a comma.)

■ *Introductory expressions, phrases, clauses* — Commas follow introductory words, phrases, and clauses unless the phrase or clause is very short.

EXAMPLES:

Yes, we can arrange a conference call tomorrow.

In addition, the Stockton case has been postponed.

By the way, mention to Carl that I need his Prost figures.

Before you leave on Friday, give Fran your itinerary.

By tomorrow we should be in Florida. (Short phrase requires no comma.)

■ *Setting off nonessential or descriptive material* — Commas separate nonessential or descriptive material from the rest of the sentence. Such expressions or descriptions can be dropped from the sentence without changing the meaning.

EXAMPLES:

Boston Limited, headquartered in Maine, recently introduced a product similar to ours. (The material set off with commas is incidental information.)

■ Such expressions as *for example, for instance, in my opinion, on the contrary, of course* are set off by commas whether they are placed at the beginning, middle, or end of the sentence.

EXAMPLES:

For example, the air freight costs alone will reduce our profit margin by 5 percent.

I agree, of course, that we must reach a decision soon.

I'm not sure I can send the brochure by Friday, however.

■ *Direct address*—Occasionally you will address your recipients directly in your memo. Set off their names with commas regardless of where in the sentence the names appear.

EXAMPLES:

When you find the data on Conco, Howard, call me.

Bernice, we need to reorganize the menu for next week.

Will you forward my mail to the conference site, Al?

■ *Names, dates, addresses, numbers*—Commas are used to separate elements in names, dates, addresses, and numbers.

EXAMPLES:

Dan O'Rourke, Jr. Judith Turpin, Ph.D. Ms. Ling, Manager

The deadline has been set for May 12, 1992. (However, no commas are used with only the month and year: May 1992.)

Their company's new address is Lankowitz & Hardy, 443 Market Street, San Francisco, CA 94112.

We paid $14 per share for 12,000 shares of United.

Semicolon. A stronger break in a sentence than a comma, semicolons are not as complete a break as a period or colon. They have two functions.

■ *Joining two complete thoughts*—Semicolons join two closely related complete thoughts when such linking words as *and, but, for, or, nor, yet* are not used.

EXAMPLES:

The copier has been in use for six months; so far it has performed perfectly.

I understand your hesitation about the loan; however, Kalid's credit record is excellent.

■ *Separating complete thoughts or items in a series that contain internal punctuation.* In some cases, one of two complete thoughts — or one or more items in a series — will contain commas. Semicolons are used to help the reader understand which information goes with which part.

EXAMPLES:

In my opinion, Neal should be promoted; and I know Grace Asland would agree.

Their top executives are Fashim Said, Finance; Demmie Yale, Marketing; Vera Teas, Legal Affairs; and Marilyn Nunn, CEO.

Colon.   Colons represent a more complete stop than a semicolon but not as full a stop as a period. They are used before a series or list, between two complete thoughts, in expressions of time, and after the introductory and closing headings in a memo.

■ *Before a series or list* — As discussed in Chapter 4, colons can be used to introduce a series or list to add white space to a memo. Colons are used only after complete thoughts, before introducing a series, or after such expressions as *the following* or *as follows* to introduce a bulleted or numbered list.

INCORRECT:

I have the latest demographics for: New York, Philadelphia, Boston, and Hartford. (*I have the latest demographics for* is not a complete thought. The colon should be omitted.)

CORRECT:

I have the latest demographics for four eastern cities: New York, Philadelphia, Boston, and Hartford.

Dun & Bradstreet sent us corporate data on the following:

New York Mutual Life

Northwestern Mutual

Washington National

Bradford Assurance

■ *Between two complete thoughts* — Like semicolons, colons can separate two complete thoughts when such linking words as *and, but, or, nor, yet* are not used. The second complete thought can begin with either a lower case or capital letter.

EXAMPLES:

Ted has a solution to our problem: ship the parts by truck.

I have only one question: Can we make the June 1 deadline?

■ *Numerical expressions of time* — Colons are used when writing time in number form. Do not use the words *o'clock* with numbered time expressions.

INCORRECT:

The flight leaves at 5:00 o'clock P.M.

We scheduled a 2:00 o'clock meeting for Tuesday.

CORRECT:

The flight leaves at 5:00 P.M. *or* The flight leaves at 5:00 in the evening.

The mayor will see us at 12:00 noon.

When expressing international or military time in *figures*, place colons between the hours and minutes and between minutes and seconds.

EXAMPLES:

04:30 (4:30 in the morning)

16:30 (4:30 in the afternoon)

16:30:02 (sixteen hours, thirty minutes, and two seconds past midnight)

■ *After introductory and closing headings* — Colons follow all introductory and closing headings in a memo and between the initials of the sender and typist.

EXAMPLES:

To: Constance Gervais, Manager   Date: August 8, 19—

From: Angus Shofield   Reference: Order 344

Subject: PURCHASE ORDER FOR GATEWAYS BOOKS

AJS:rj

cc: Adam Berteau

Quotation marks. Quotation marks are used to enclose a direct quotation, titles of articles and other publications, and unusual terms and expressions.

■ *Punctuation with quotation marks* — Most writers have trouble remembering how to use punctuation with quotation marks. The guidelines are fairly simple.

1. Periods and commas are *always* placed *inside* the closing quotation marks.

2. Semicolons and colons are always placed *outside* the closing quotation marks.

3. Question marks and exclamation points are placed *inside* the closing quotation marks *only* if they are part of the quoted material. Otherwise they are placed *outside* the quotation marks.

4. Only *one* punctuation mark is used at the end of a sentence. (Have you read "What Next for Corporate America?" The question mark applies to the title and to the sentence.)

EXAMPLES:

Commas and Periods

Lou claims we are "six months short," but I don't agree.

Take a look at Carla's article, "Six Ways to Increase Your Chances for Promotion."

Semicolons and Colons

The item should be listed under "HMOs"; if you don't find it there, look under "Health maintenance organizations."

The following have been classified as "wholly owned subsidiaries": Piermont Trucking, Fancy Dan's, CompuShop, and Jade Florist.

Question Marks and Exclamation Points

Did the contract read "all North American rights" or "all world rights"? (The question mark punctuates the sentence.)

I have already read "Which Way Corporate America?" (The question mark punctuates the title only; no other punctuation mark is needed for the sentence.)

Attached is a copy of "Supercomputing in 2001!" which I mentioned to you. (The exclamation point punctuates the title.)

We're ranked number four in the *Fortune* "500"! (The exclamation point punctuates the entire sentence.)

■ *Direct quotation* — Quotation marks are used to enclose someone's exact words.

EXAMPLES:

I think he said that our department was showing the entire company how to be efficient. (The writer is paraphrasing a quote.)

He said our department "is a model of efficiency for the entire company." (The writer reproduces the exact wording.)

■ Quoted material running over two lines should be indented and single-spaced in the memo. No quote marks are used.

EXAMPLE:

He said the following:

> The Finance Department is a model of efficiency for the entire company. Their productivity rating is three times higher than any other department, and they consistently meet or exceed their goals.

■ *Titles* — Quotation marks enclose the titles of articles, reports, many business and government publications, and chapters of books. Titles are set off by commas from the rest of the sentence unless they serve as the subject of the sentence.

EXAMPLES:

I found the chapter, "Lessons of Leadership," particularly helpful.

"Transatlantic Communications" was written by one of our colleagues. (The article title is the subject of the sentence and does not require a comma.)

Please send me the government's study, "The Graying of Our American Work Force."

■ *Unusual terms and expressions* — unusual or unfamiliar terms and expressions used in your memo may be enclosed in quotation marks. However, keep such words to a minimum.

EXAMPLES:

We can insert a "grandfather clause" into our Chicago lease.

Did he say "ROM" or "RAM" cards could boost our computer power?

His recommendation to "ride the tiger" on this stock sounds too risky to me.

Apostrophe. The apostrophe is used to form contractions, to show possession, and to form the plural of numbers and symbols.

■ *Contractions* — In contractions, the apostrophe takes the place of missing letters.

EXAMPLES:

do not = don't	it has/is = it's	they are = they're
have not = haven't	I will = I'll	who has/is = who's

NOTE: Do not confuse the contraction *it's* with the possessive pronoun *its*. (The company is selling *its* stock. *It's* [it has] sold stock through the NYSE.)

■ *Possession* — The apostrophe, along with the letter *s*, forms the possessive of singular and plural nouns and certain pronouns.

1. To form the possessive of a singular noun, add an apostrophe and an *s*. Words or names that end in a *z* sound may take only an apostrophe at the end to avoid too many *s* sounds.

EXAMPLES:

the company's inventory   Barbara's records

the product's market share   Alice Burns' resume

2. To form the possessive of a plural noun ending in *s*, add only the apostrophe. Nouns that are already plural (e.g., women, men) take *'s*.

EXAMPLES:

the assistants' salaries   children's wear

3. Pronouns such as *everyone, no one, someone* require *'s* to form the possessive. Personal pronouns do not take an apostrophe.

EXAMPLES:

The error was no one's fault.   The fault is **hers**.

Everyone's sticker has expired.   **His** sticker expired.

4. Joint possession is shown by adding an *'s* to the last word or name.

EXAMPLES:

Nancy and Andy's report (the report belongs to both)

Procter & Gamble's stock

5. In individual possession, both nouns or pronouns take *'s* or an apostrophe only.

EXAMPLES:

Nancy's and Andy's reports (both people have reports)

the vice-president's and secretary's letters

6. Words such as *minute, hour, day, week, year, cents, dollars,* etc., take an apostrophe or *'s* when used as possessives.

EXAMPLES:

one day's notice   three weeks' pay

a minute's time   ten minutes' work

a year's grace   five years' earnings

■ *Plural form of numbers and symbols* — Always use *'s* to form the plural of numbers and symbols.

EXAMPLES:

The answers are coded with T's and F's.

The number 3's look fuzzy on this page.

They're changing all the #'s to +'s in the next form.

Hyphens.
Hyphens are used with spelled-out numbers, some prefixes and suffixes, and compound adjectives before a noun, and to avoid misreading words.

■ *Spelled-out numbers* — use a hyphen with numbers from twenty-one to ninety-nine and with fractions used as an adjective.

EXAMPLES:

twenty-nine typewriters   a three-fourths majority

                                        But: three fourths of the employees
                                        "three fourths" is a noun

■ *Prefixes and suffixes* — Prefixes *ex-, all-, self-* and the suffix *-elect* always use a hyphen. All prefixes before proper nouns and adjectives also take a hyphen.

EXAMPLES:

self-esteem   president-elect   pro-Canadian

ex-officer   all-Korean team   Pan-American

■ *Compound adjectives* — Adjectives formed from two words are joined by a hyphen when they come before the noun but not when they follow the noun. However, when one word ends in *-ly*, no hyphens are used.

EXAMPLES:

city-owned business	*but*	wholly owned subsidiary
decision-making process	*but*	a process of decision making
a past-due bill	*but*	a bill that is past due

■ *Avoiding confusion* — Use hyphens to prevent confusion or awkwardness in your writing.

EXAMPLES:

re-creation	(avoids confusion with *recreation*)
sub-subentry	(avoids awkwardness of *subsubentry*)
re-evaluation	(avoids awkwardness of *reevaluation*)

Subject—Verb Agreement

The basic rule of subject—verb agreement is simple: a singular subject (desk) takes a singular verb (The desk *is* expensive.); a plural subject (desks) takes a plural verb (The desks *are* expensive.).

But it is not always easy to tell when a subject is singular or plural. The guidelines that follow will help you to select the right verb for the subject.

■ *Compound subjects joined by* and — Subjects joined by *and* (three stocks *and* four bonds) are called "compound subjects." They take a singular or plural verb depending on the circumstances.

1. *Singular verb* — Compound subjects joined by *and* take a singular verb when (a) the subject is considered a unit (research and development), and (b) when both parts of the verb are modified by *each* or *every*.

EXAMPLES:

Finance and accounting was given a budget increase this year.

Each computer and *every* printer *has* a surge protector.

NOTE: The exception to this rule involves the word *all*. When used with a singular noun *all* requires a singular verb (*All* of the *paper is* missing.). When used with a plural noun, it takes a plural verb (*All* of the *papers are* missing.).

2. *Plural verb* — Compound subjects joined by *and* take a plural verb even when one of the subjects is singular.

EXAMPLES:

The Ohio plant and the *Houston foundry were* sold.

Three accountants and *two IRS agents say* they will testify on our behalf.

One company car and *three trucks are* available for use.

■ *Compound subjects joined by* or *or* nor. The rules for compound subjects joined by *or* or *nor* are slightly more complicated.

1. *Singular verbs* — If the subject next to the verb is singular or if both parts of the subject are singular, then the verb is singular as well.

EXAMPLES:

Neither *Al* nor *Hannah knows* what happened to the memo.

Has the *copier* or the *fax machine* broken down?

Either the *safety deposit boxes* or *the vault is* a good place to store your valuables. (The subject closest to the verb is singular.)

2. *Plural verb* — If both subjects joined by *or* or *nor* are plural, or if the subject nearest the verb is plural, then use a plural verb.

EXAMPLES:

Tell me if *the secretaries* or *the assistants are* going to handle travel arrangements.

Either *the vault* or *the safety deposit boxes are* a good place to store your valuables.

■ *Collective nouns* — Collective nouns (*staff, management, board of directors*) take either a singular or plural verb depending on the context of your sentences. If you emphasize the group as a unit, use a singular verb. If you emphasize the individuals within the group, use a plural verb.

EXAMPLES:

The board of directors *has* voted on the takeover bid. (Here the board is viewed as a group.)

The board of directors *disagree* about the takeover bid. (Here the board is viewed as individuals.)

Management *rejects* the union's proposed settlement.

The company's top management *are* certain a settlement can be reached.

■ *Measurements* — All measurements (dollars, miles, pounds, centimeters, grams) take a singular verb.

EXAMPLES:

Is $12 million their highest offer?

Fifty miles is the average distance between delivery sites.

Does thirty pounds per package sound too high to you?

■ *Words modifying the subject* — Material following the subject or set off by commas can make it difficult to determine if the subject is singular or plural. Simply block out the additional material and look only at the subject to decide on the correct verb form.

EXAMPLES:

Each of the companies *has* filed for bankruptcy. (Each has)

None of the workers *is* willing to quit. (None [not one] is)

Our *products*, particularly the electronics line, *were* all successful last year. (Our products were)

Their *firm*, like several other law firms, *was* caught unprepared by the new antitrust legislation. (Firm was)

Abbreviations

Abbreviations are used in foreign terms, names and titles, units of measure, and addresses. Although traditionally abbreviations are punctuated with periods, the modern trend is to drop the periods and use only letters. Your company may have its own style, and you should follow it consistently.

■ *Common foreign terms* — The following abbreviations are used in all types of writing. Notice that *e.g.* and *i.e.* are each followed by a comma.

A.M. or a.m. (before noon)	etc. (and so forth)
P.M. or p.m. ((after noon)	e.g., (for example)
AM/am PM/pm (without periods)	i.e., (that is)

■ *Names and titles* — Because abbreviations used with government agencies, company names, and personal names vary, make sure you copy the abbreviation style exactly as the agency, company, or individual uses it.

EXAMPLES:

Government Agencies

D.O.D. (Department of Defense)

NASA (National Aeronautics and Space Administration)

HHS (Health and Human Services)

Company Names

Mott Electronics, Inc. (incorporated)

Chas R Rodgers Co (company — notice the absence of periods with the abbreviations)

Blue Island Corp. (corporation)

Haversham & Gwaine, Ltd. (limited partnership)

Personal Names and Titles

Dr. Lane	Mr. Andres	Ms. Ling
Will Lane, MD	Fred Andres, PhD	Sherry Ling, MBA
Will Lane, Jr.	Fred Andres, Sr.	Sherry Ling, Esq.

NOTE: The plural of a title is formed by adding *s* to the abbreviation or *'s* if periods are used: MBA*s*, MD*s*, Ph.D.*'s*.

■ *Units of measure* — Abbreviations of English units (feet, inches, miles, etc.) are generally written with periods, while metric units are abbreviated without periods.

EXAMPLES:

3 g (grams)   12 lbs. 4 oz.   5 kB (kilobytes)

3 ft. 2 in.   22 km (kilometers)   18 cm (centimeters)

■ *Addresses* — Abbreviations for streets, highways, expressways, avenues, and the like are generally written with periods. However, each company has its preferred style. Postal abbreviations (IL, MO, MD) never require periods.

EXAMPLES:

Blvd. (boulevard)   St. (Street)   Ave. (avenue)

AL (Alabama)   GU (Guam Islands)

A complete list of abbreviations for the United States and for foreign countries is provided in any ZIP code directory.

Capitalization

The rules for capitalization vary from company to company. Whatever style you use, be consistent. Most companies follow these guidelines:

■ *Proper names and adjectives* — Capitalize all proper names and adjectives whether they refer to persons, organizations, companies, products, or government institutions.

EXAMPLES:

Lucy Tate (proper name)   British (proper adjective)

American Hospital Association   Pepsi Cola, Inc.

Sony Walkman   Kodak Instamatic

State Department   United Nations

■ *Geographical names and regions* — Capitalize all geographic names and regions, but do not capitalize points of the compass when used simply as directions (north, south, east, west).

EXAMPLES:

New York	Northeast (region of the country)	North America
Lake Michigan	St. Lawrence Seaway	Atlantic Ocean
First Avenue	Ohio Turnpike	Route 66
Mount Fuji	Caspian Sea	Gobi Desert

■ *Seasons* — Do not capitalize the names of seasons.

EXAMPLES:

We'll begin construction in **fall** 1995.

Our **summer** sale accounted for half our profits.

■ *Titles* — Capitalize titles when they come before a person's name. When titles follow the name, they may be capitalized or lowercase. Titles used alone are generally not capitalized unless they refer to the highest offices in the government (Secretary of State, President, Vice President).

EXAMPLES:

President Ingram of Reach, Inc.	president of Reach, Inc.
Director Pauline Ryan	Pauline Ryan, Director
	or
	Pauline Ryan, director

■ *Academic degrees* are capitalized whether they come before or after a person's name or are used alone.

EXAMPLES:

Dr. Elaine Sommers   Elaine Sommers, MD
(only one title is used with the name:
not Dr. Elaine Sommers, MD)

Joseph Olesky, LLD   Laurette Coulds, BS, MBA

■ *Documents and publications* — Capitalize the first word and all important words in documents and publication titles. However, when *charter, act, treaty,* or *law* are used alone they are not capitalized.

EXAMPLES:

Uniform Commercial Code   Tax Reform Act of 1987

Declaration of Independence   International Space Treaty

In Search of Excellence (book)

"Nuclear Energy in the Third World" (article)

Washington Post (newspaper)

Congress passed the deregulation *act* on March 10.

Numbers

Numbers appear frequently in memos in the form of dates, measurements, amounts of money, percentages, fractions and decimals, and as part of an address or company name. The following guidelines are often used in business writing:

■ *Words or figures*—When do you use figures or words to express numbers? Follow these rules.

1. Spell out numbers ten and under; use figures for higher numbers. Large round numbers can be spelled out (two thousand) or written in words and figures ($12 million, 25 million gallons).

2. Avoid starting a sentence with a number. Either spell out the number or reword the sentence.

Poor: 27 cases had been damaged in the accident.
Better: Twenty-seven cases had been damaged in the accident.
Poor: 1987 marked the first year of our new venture.
Better: In 1987, we began our new venture. *or* Our new venture began in 1987.

3. Use figures to express sums of money, but use words for small sums serving as adjectives.

EXAMPLES:

Waterson estimated each transaction would cost *$4,500.*

According to my calculations, we have a *$45.60* refund coming.

The company charges a *five-dollar* fee for direct mail.

■ *Words and figures together*—When two numbers referring to different measures follow one another in the same sentence, the smaller number is expressed in words.

EXAMPLES:

Martin ordered *400 twenty-inch* cables.

Martin ordered *six 20-inch* cables.

Do you have *25 ten-cent* stamps?

No, I have only *eight 15-cent* stamps.

■ *Numbers in a series* — If any number in a series is over ten, all the numbers should be expressed as figures. If all numbers are under ten, they are expressed in words.

EXAMPLES:

The order specified *5* boxes of pens, *24* reams of paper, *13* memo pads, and *7* toner cartridges.

The order specified *five* boxes of pens, *three* reams of paper, *two* memo pads, and *seven* toner cartridges.

■ *Addresses* — Words are used for numbered street names *one* through *ten*. Separate address number and street name with a hyphen preceded and followed by one space. Use numbers for all state and federal highways.

EXAMPLES:

One South Arlington St.	377 *Fifth* Avenue
117-23d Street	*1921-119th* Avenue
U.S. Route *1*	Illinois *94*

■ *Dates* — Dates are expressed as month/day/year or day/month/ year, depending on the style used. When month and day or simply the day is used, the date can be written in figures or in words.

EXAMPLES:

My vacation begins on *June 10, 1992.*
or
My vacation begins on *10 June 1992.* (Notice with the day/month/ year arrangement, no comma separates the month and year.)

Our fiscal year ends on *September 30* (September 30th).
or
Our fiscal year ends on the *thirtieth of September.*

We issue payroll checks on the *fifteenth* of every month.

or

We issue payroll checks on the *15th* of every month.

■ *Money*—Amounts in round numbers are written without the decimal and zeros. If other money amounts in the sentence use decimals, however, make sure all amounts are written consistently. For amounts under a dollar, use figures and the word *cents*.

EXAMPLES:

We can purchase their stock for *$23* per share.

The three stocks sold for *$22.00*, *$19.75*, and *$6.25*, respectively.

If we order 500 floppy diskettes, they will cost only 25 *cents* apiece.

■ *Percentages, fractions, decimals*—Percentages are expressed in figures with the word *percent*. (However, the symbol % is used in tables and charts.) Mixed fractions and decimals are written in figures, although simple fractions can be expressed in words.

EXAMPLES:

Inflation rose only *1.3 percent* in the fourth quarter.

12 1/4 in. by *15 3/4* in.   *one-half* share of the market

6.25 centimeters   *two thirds* completed

456.7 kilometers

0.19 grams

■ *Titles*—Numbers used in company names or official titles of events can be expressed either in numbers or words. Copy the company's or organization's style accurately.

EXAMPLES:

First Community Savings   *1st* National Bank

Third Rockaway Marathon   *5th* Chili Bakeoff

XXV Summer Olympiad

PROOFREAD YOUR MEMO

After going through the review checklist and grammar points, carefully proofread your final copy. If you have time, let someone else proof it as well. These steps are important even if you write your memos on computer. A computer "spellcheck" program will catch spelling errors but not mistakes in grammar, word choice, dates, figures, or times in your memo.

For example, in the sentence, "We have ordered *there* rebuilt printer heads," a spellcheck program will skip right over the correctly spelled *there* without noticing it should be *three*.

The best way to proofread your message is to read it systematically. For example, look at all the names first and double-check their spelling. Then check all the figures, then all your headings, lists, and so on. By working through your message systematically, you are far more likely to catch errors than if you tried to look for everything in one reading.

Proofing marks commonly used follow. They make your corrections easier to read and are recognized by most typists and word processors.

ℓ	delete	⟨tr⟩ ⌒	transpose
⌒	close up space	sp	spell out
ℛ	delete and close up	stet	let it stand
#	leave space	ℓc	lowercase letter
¶	begin new paragraph	C	capital letter
↶⍪ /	insert comma	⩘/	insert semicolon
⩙ ⩙/	insert apostrophe	⩘/	insert colon
"/"	insert quotation marks	=/	insert hyphen
⊙	insert period	⊥/m	insert dash
?/	insert question mark	(/)	insert parentheses
no ¶. Run in.	run paragraphs together	[/]	insert brackets

Compare the proofread and corrected memos below.

Original:

To: Anton Roundtree, Vice President, Production

⩘/ From| Patricia Farkas, Human Resources

⟨tr⟩ Date: March 32, 1991

Subject: CANDIDATE FOR QUALITY CONTROL MANAGER

of the four candidates |ve interviewed for quality control manager, only /⩙

one—Karin Voorhees|meets our criteria. /⊥m

No ¶. Run in. His resume and Letters of recomendation are attached. ℓc

My impression of Mr. Voorhees is one of a dedicated, hard working

manager with ~~a lot of~~ *considerable* experience in robotics. On the basis of his

excellent qualifications, I strongly recommend him for the (mgt)

position. He also shows a keen understanding of our quality control

problems. If you agree he is a likely candidate for the job, I can

arrange for you to interview him next week.

Corrected:

To: Anton Roundtree, Vice President, Production
From: Patricia Farkas, Human Resources
Date: March 23, 1991
Subject: CANDIDATE FOR QUALITY CONTROL MANAGER

Of the four candidates I've interviewed for quality control manager,
only one—Karin Voorhees—meets our criteria. His resume and letters
of recommendation are attached.

My impression of Mr. Voorhees is one of a dedicated, hardworking
manager with considerable experience in robotics. He also shows a
keen understanding of our quality control problems. On the basis of his
excellent qualifications, I strongly recommend him for the management
position.

If you agree he is a likely candidate for the job, I can arrange for you to
interview him next week.

SUMMARY

■ The review process is a critical step in your writing. It is your
last chance to make sure you have answered the four key
questions, crafted your language, checked your grammar and your
facts, and proofread the final version for careless errors.

■ Use the review checklist to ensure that your memos are as clear, concise, and accurate as possible.

1. Is the memo format completed correctly?
2. Have I stated my purpose clearly?
3. Have I analyzed my readers?
4. Have I determined the scope and meaning of my topic?
5. Have I stated clearly what response I want from the reader?
6. Is my memo well organized?
7. Have I varied my sentence length and construction?
8. Have I made good use of white space and emphasis devices?
9. Is my language vivid and concise?

■ Use the grammar guidelines in this book to check your grammar usage. Keep a good dictionary, thesaurus, and grammar book on hand to answer your questions about punctuation, verb forms, subject—verb agreement, abbreviations, capitalization, numbers, spelling, and word choice.

■ Proofread your memo by going through the message systematically to catch any errors.

MEMOS AND THE ELECTRONIC OFFICE

▼

"Stan, have you got the blueprints on hand for that Howard Street office building?" Lorraine asked.

"They're right here in the file. Why?"

"The New York office needs a copy along with my memo report for a three o'clock meeting. I want to fax the package to them by noon."

Stan laughed. "Remember the good old days? One of us would have to hop the next flight to New York and deliver the material in person."

The secretary was apologetic. "I'm sorry, Mr. Walsh, but Ms. Carlson is out of the office until tomorrow morning. Can I have her call you back then?"

"No, I'll be at the Avery site tomorrow morning. I tell you what, all I need are some construction estimates from her. I'll just leave a memo."

Walsh called up the memo form from his electronic mail file and typed in his request on the form. He sent the memo to Carlson's electronic mailbox so that it would be waiting for her in the morning.

The following day, when Carlson saw the memo from Walsh, she filled in the construction estimates in the section of the form marked "Reply." She made a copy of the memo, filing it under "Avery," then sent the memo back to Walsh's electronic mailbox. That afternoon, Walsh retrieved his memo with Carlson's answer and was able to complete his construction proposal to the Avery corporation.

OFFICE AUTOMATION SYSTEMS, or OAS, give business an un-dreamed-of flexibility in communications. These systems include local area networks (LANs) and electronic message systems. Today's memo writers can send a memo electronically across the hall or across an ocean in seconds or minutes. If communications technology is creating the "global village," putting us all instantaneously in touch with one another, it is also making the "global office" a reality.

Regardless of the sophisticated hardware and software used, how-ever, the *message* is still the most important element in the equation. The lightning speed of electronic communications makes it even more imperative that your message be clear, concise, and accurate. As every manager knows, once a mistake enters a communications network, cor-recting it can be a frustrating, time-consuming experience.

LOCAL AREA NETWORKS — THE NEW OFFICE LAN-SCAPE

Local area networks, or LANs, are based on a simple principle: a computer capable of communicating with other computers is more valu-able than one standing alone. LAN communications networks generally share a server or host computer and a printer. Local area networks can operate within the confines of a single department, a single building, or over an area of several square miles, connecting several offices. Although LANs are capable of long-distance data transmission, their basic function is to increase productivity and flexibility among a local group of office workers.

This fact makes LANs ideal for the memo writer. Instead of creating a paper memo, the user can create an electronic message and send it to each LAN member. Recipients can place their comments or replies on the electronic memo and return it to the sender within minutes. In fact, LANs are so convenient that companies should make sure that their networks aren't encouraging the overuse of memos instead of streamlining communications.

LAN Configurations

LANs vary widely in shared computing power, intelligence, methods and speed of transmission, and basic layouts. The most common layouts are hub or star, bus line, ring, mesh, and tree or hierarchy, as shown in Exhibit 6–1. *Hub* or *star networks* are the simplest to develop. All communications pass through a central processing device or host computer. *Bus line networks* consist basically of a string of terminals connected to a single cable. In theory, an unlimited number of terminals can be added to the cable, depending on the user's needs.

Ring networks involve linking a group of computers to one another, with automation devices tied into each personal computer. These net-

Exhibit 6–1. LAN Configurations

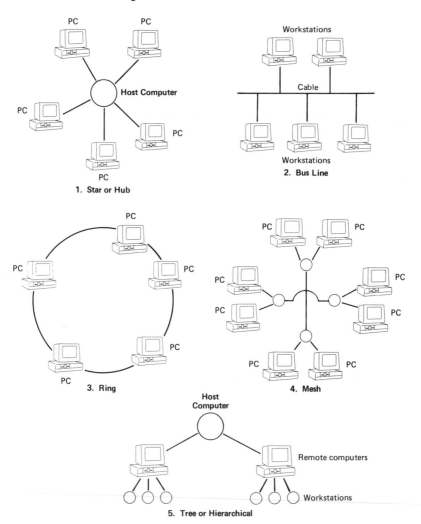

works are relatively inexpensive to establish and provide an alternate route should service be lost at any point in the ring. *Mesh networks* allow any two devices within a network to communicate directly. This type of configuration provides multiple routes in and out of each location.

Finally, *tree* or *hierarchical networks* are built in levels, beginning with a host or server computer. At the second level, micro or personal computers connect directly into the host computer, unlike the ring network in which they are linked to one another. In turn, at the third level, other automated devices can be tied into each personal computer, creating a mini-LAN.

How LANs Operate

In many cases, each employee has a personal computer, or PC, with the ability to create, store, and retrieve files. The main computing power, however, comes from the host computer. The host computer stores data that can be used by several people in the network at once. The users often share other devices, such as printers, fax machines, and copiers. They can send documents to the printer, which takes printing jobs in the order they are received.

In other cases, employees may have "diskless computers," that is, computers with no hard or floppy disks of their own. Data files are stored exclusively in a central data bank or in the host computer. Companies can keep control over sensitive information, because no one can make a disk copy of their files. At the same time, everyone with the proper access code can use the files when needed. Insurance companies, direct mail order houses, and publishers of multivolume texts, such as encyclopedias, often use diskless computers in their operations.

Advantages and Disadvantages

LANs have several advantages that make them ideal for large or small companies alike.

■ They speed up communications and work flow and increase productivity. LANs eliminate the need for workers to pass paper copies or disks back and forth, risking damage or loss of data files.
■ They enable users to have access to common files. This access means more than one person can work with the same data, such as sales figures. Documents can be seen by a greater number of people at the same time.

■ Diskless PCs tend to be more reliable than standard personal computers, and they help companies control access to sensitive information.

The main disadvantages of LANs are related to limitations in hardware and software and to operator errors.

■ If the host computer breaks down or has problems, so will all the computers on the network. Smooth, continuous operation of the host computer is critical.

■ Lack of standardized equipment can cause problems when LAN users from one department want to send information to LAN users in another department. Format codes and complex data may not be received exactly as they were sent.

■ Errors made by individual users can affect everyone on the network. If an error is not caught, everyone will base his/her work on one individual's incorrect data.

■ Policies and procedures for LAN use must be carefully established and taught to workers. Sloppy use of the network can be disastrous for everyone.

ELECTRONIC MAIL

Electronic mail (e-mail) can beam information anywhere, from across the hall to halfway around the world, instantaneously. E-mail operates through computer-to-computer links or through facsimile machines, telex, teletex, TWR, and even the telegram. Signals can be sent either over common-carrier phone lines or via satellite relays. E-mail is ideally adapted for use in local area networks. Some of the more common ways of moving e-mail include facsimile machines, document distribution through communicating word processors, and electronic message systems.

Fax Machines

A facsimile or fax machine has become one of the fastest-growing components of office automation. Its widespread use has even spawned a new verb—to fax. In its most basic form, the fax machine can be thought of as a supercopier with data communications facilities. Fax devices come in three types: stand-alone transmitters, stand-alone receivers, and combined transmitters and receivers—all operating at one of several speeds.

Although the facsimile process was originally developed in the 1800s, it has been continually refined. In general, fax machines are categorized as Group 1, Group 2, Group 3, or, more recently, Group 4. Group 1 is the oldest and slowest of the four, while Group 4 includes prototypes of smart fax machines. The modern facsimile process consists of five steps, as shown in Exhibit 6–2.

- A document scanner called the transmitter converts an image into electrical signals.
- These signals are modulated for transmission through telephone lines, often via a built-in modem, to another fax machine at a remote location.
- The electrical signals are demodulated at the receiving end.
- A receiver reconverts the signals and prints out a hard-copy form of the image. This version is regarded as a "facsimile" of the original.
- The receiving fax machine sends a message back to the sending machine confirming that the entire message was received.

Exhibit 6–2. FAX Transmission and Reception

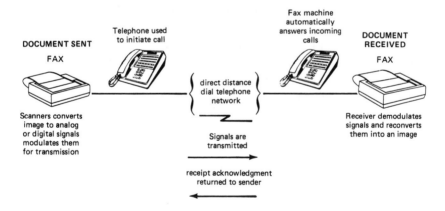

Transmission speeds vary from several minutes per page to only a few seconds, depending on whether analog or digital signals are used. With analog, each signal represents a complete document, white space and all. The image is divided into picture elements, or *pixels*, with a signal for each element. Although slower than digital, analog signals produce sharper, clearer images.

In digital processing, only actual image content is converted into binary information (zeros and ones). Through a coding scheme, the image is compressed both horizontally and vertically, which permits faster transmission times. Overall, digital facsimile is more efficient and lends itself to use with a computer or computer network. Fax equipment also has optional capabilities, such as automatic dial, automatic answer, and automatic disconnect. The more recently developed smart fax machines can negotiate with one another about the priority of their messages and the quality of their connection. They then adjust their transmission speeds accordingly.

Advantages and disadvantages. The primary advantage of the fax machine is that the contents of any page — text, drawings, photos, handwritten material — can be transmitted. This capability is particularly useful when you need to send supporting documents or attachments with a memo, such as blueprints, schematics, photos, illustrations, or art layouts.

Also, no keyboard data entry is required. The only manual operation necessary involves feeding source material into the machine and, on the receiving end, collecting the printed pages. Finally, fax equipment is relatively inexpensive and easy to install and operate wherever telephone lines will work. No special room is required. These advantages make fax machines ideal for an office that does not have LANs or sophisticated computer equipment to transmit e-mail. Companies have found that faxing documents, such as memos, is considerably cheaper than sending them via overnight mail.

The main disadvantage of fax machines is that image fidelity and reliability depend on the quality of the hardware and signal transmission and reception. If anything disrupts the signals, such as a breakdown on the telephone lines, the receiver may not get the entire transmission. Also, as many managers are discovering, anyone with your fax number can send you information, whether you want it or not. Finally, security is usually low. Fax machines are often placed in the copier room and are accessible to anyone in the company. Thus, managers who send and receive confidential information may have a fax machine in their own offices.

Although fax machines are usually stand-alone devices, the practice of linking them with computer-based electronic mail has been increasing over the past few years. Industry experts anticipate that as fax machines get faster, smarter, and cheaper, this trend will continue.

Document Distribution

Document distribution involves using communicating word processors, such as those in a network, to transmit a document to any network user. Documents can be exchanged by moving the document to the destination; storing it in a central repository, such as a host computer; or a combination of both methods. Memos generated by one network user can thus be sent to one or all of the other users and stored on their individual PCs, in the central data bank, or in both.

In most cases, the heart of the document distribution system is a mail log maintained by electronic mail software. Users log onto the system by entering an assigned password or number and receive a log on the screen that gives information for current electronic mail: item number, date, author, description of the item, whether it is outgoing or incoming, and its state of processing.

Document distribution also allows users to send a document, such as a memo, to a distribution list; redistribute the document; and append a reply to the original before returning it. Users can send abbreviated memos back and forth quickly to get answers to questions, to set a meeting agenda, and so on. This application of electronic mail can facilitate communication among workers located on separate floors in an office building or in different office sites.

Electronic Message Systems

Electronic message systems technology has evolved from telegraph, Teletype, telex/TWX, and finally computer-based, or interpersonal, message systems (CBMS or IPMS). The objective of IPMS systems is to improve office productivity and not to produce documents for outside distribution. The basic function of an IPMS is to handle text, as in word processing. It allows messages to be created, filed, transmitted, and retrieved. It also facilitates communication by providing such features as generalized documents and forms, distribution lists, reply, and search functions.

A user who wishes to create and send a memo, for example, logs onto the e-mail program and selects the company's memo form available from several predefined document forms stored in the host computer. The memo form is displayed on the screen along with information lines, such as recipient, sender, date, subject line, return receipt, distribution list, and so on.

Once the memo is created, the sender keys in who should receive it and sends it out electronically. The memo is stored in individual users' electronic mailboxes, which each user checks periodically. The sender can keep a copy of the memo by creating a file and storing it in the host computer or on a disk. The user then logs off the e-mail program. When users next sign on to their e-mail systems, they first check their electronic mailboxes for any incoming messages waiting to be read.

IPMS are often implemented through a computer network because they can easily be piggybacked onto a data processing network. The success of an IPMS depends on the integration of data processing, word processing, and electronic mail. Exhibit 6–3 shows what an integrated office automation system might look like with LANs, IPMS, and fax machines. Such a system can be used to distribute memos within a LAN, between one office and another, or from one continent to another. The office is fully integrated within and connected to the outside world via its communications linkups.

Voicemail. A more recent development in electronic message systems is known as "voicemail." These systems combine the convenience of answering machines with the functions of a computer. When you are out of the office, incoming callers will automatically be connected to your voicemail system. The caller can leave a recorded message in your voicemail box. You then dial into the system to pick up your messages.

Such a system can eliminate telephone tag in which callers continually miss one another. Because most studies show that many business calls are simply to convey information *one way*, voicemail can save companies time and money.

The system can also be efficient in another way. "Voice memos" can be recorded and distributed to several voicemail boxes, eliminating the need to send a paper memo or to call people individually.

The major drawbacks with voicemail involve its cost and workers' perception of the system. Unless the system is accepted by employees, it will be seen as unreliable and too much trouble to use.

Advantages and disadvantages. The major advantages of electronic message systems are as follows:

■ They greatly reduce the time between the creation of a message and its reception. Previously, the message originated in a manager's office, was sent to word processing, and then transmitted to recipients. The sender then had to wait for a reply. Today, the message can be sent through a network or over the manager's modem or fax machine and a reply received the same day.

■ The systems overcome time-zone differences and eliminate delays due to weekends, holidays, and evenings after business hours because messages can be delivered instantaneously.

■ They increase worker productivity and make internal communications more efficient.

Exhibit 6–3. Integrated Office Automation System

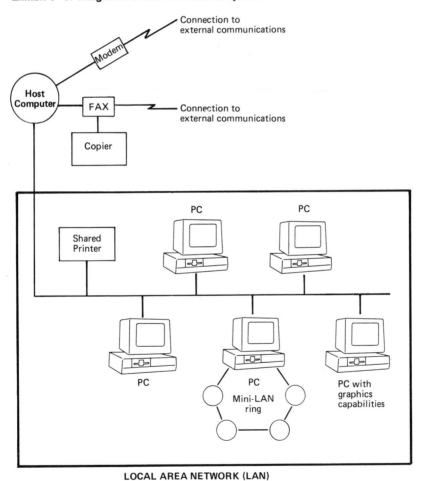

LOCAL AREA NETWORK (LAN)

But no system is without its drawbacks. The disadvantages of electronic message systems center around incompatible systems and lack of standardized equipment as well as what many companies call "skewed use"; that is, some employees use IPMS heavily while others barely use it at all. If workers are not carefully taught how to key in instructions to create, send, save, and retrieve data and to check their electronic or voicemail boxes regularly, they tend to view the system as too inconvenient. Also, workers must be careful to back up their memo files and periodically purge them to keep their correspondence in good order.

MEMOS AND OFFICE AUTOMATION

In many ways, OAS requires greater communication and organizational skills from people than did the old ways of communicating. You need to ensure the accuracy and clarity of your messages and to establish clear procedures for filing memos.

Many people have had the unsettling experience of receiving and saving an important communication, only to forget under what name or label they filed it. Retrieving the data involves a time-consuming search of disks or files that defeats the purpose of electronic message systems: to increase productivity by speeding up the communication process.

Guidelines for Memo Writing/Filing

A few guidelines can help you to keep your electronic correspondence in good working order. As you follow these guidelines, you may find yourself developing a better understanding of your job and the information flow you must handle.

Five functions. You need to perform five basic functions on incoming electronic correspondence. These functions are a more sophisticated version of handling paper memos.

1. *Read the memo and determine your response as soon as possible*—whether you need to answer, follow instructions, or simply file the memo away. In many cases, the memo form will provide a "Reply" section for your response.

Generally, if your response is longer than two pages, it is better to send it through interoffice (paper) mail than through the e-mail systems. Longer documents are easier to read on paper than on screen.

2. *You must decide how to file the memo if it needs to be saved for future reference.* As many managers have discovered, organizing files is not as easy as it may sound. Think about the main activities or functions of your job that can provide useful file headings: the clients you handle, employees you supervise, projects you are directing, data you routinely handle, and so on.

Once you have established your main functional headings, you can decide on subfile headings to make the memos easier to file and to retrieve. For example, if you are the sales manager, you might establish a main file heading with subfiles under it:

Mobile phone sales (main file heading)

January sales (subfile heading)

February sales

3. *You must be able to retrieve the file.* This means not only keeping a record of how you file memos, but knowing *where* you file them. If you have a diskless PC, you will automatically save the file to the host computer.

But PCs with their own floppy or hard disks present another problem. You must also label the disk so that you know what files are on it. You may want to print out the directory of the disk and insert it in the disk sleeve. In that way you have only to look at the directory printout to know what files are on the disk.

4. *Conduct periodic housecleaning of files.* Do you really need to save that 1986 memo about company parking lots? This step is the electronic equivalent of clearing out your paper files. Some systems may do so automatically by date or by subject. It's a good idea to make electronic housecleaning part of your work routine to keep your files and disks from becoming clogged with outdated and unnecessary communications.

5. *Back up important memos that you need to save.* Again, some systems will create backup files automatically, but many don't. Make sure you have copied important correspondence onto another disk or into a permanent file in the host computer.

Distribution. Distribution of your e-mail memos is a matter of electronically generating a routing slip. The computer can be instructed to send a copy of the memo to all those on your slip. If you have several memos to send, you may be able to instruct the computer on which messages are high priority and should be sent first. You can also forward a memo you have received to someone you think should see it.

Many e-mail software packages are developing more features that allow users to comment in the margins of memos, add their own comments in highlighted text, or even append illustrations or spreadsheets.

Confidential Memos

If you need to send a confidential memo, the old ways may be best: hand-delivering the message or putting it on a floppy disk and delivering the disk to the recipient. LANs and e-mail are by their nature meant to include, not exclude, people from the communications link.

In a computer network, for example, any memo stored in the host computer can be retrieved by someone who knows — or cracks — the access code. In addition, the system administrator cannot be locked out of any file. Thus, no confidential memos should be stored on shared media.

SUMMARY

■ Local area networks (LANs) are a group of individual personal computers sharing a host computer, printer, and other automation devices. Their purpose is to increase productivity and flexibility among a local group of workers.

■ LANs vary widely in computing power, intelligence, methods and speed of transmission, and basic layouts. The most common layouts are hub or star, bus line, ring, mesh, and tree or hierarchical.

■ Advantages of LANs include: (a) faster communications and work flow, (b) access to common files, and (c) company control of access to sensitive information through diskless PCs.

■ Disadvantages include (a) problems with the host computer or the LAN controller affecting all computers on the network, (b) lack of standardized or truly compatible equipment and software, (c) errors by individual users affecting everyone on the network, and (d) careless use of the network.

■ Electronic mail (e-mail) can beam information anywhere from across the hall to across an ocean instantaneously. E-mail is sent via fax machines, document distribution through communicating word processors, and electronic message systems.

■ Fax machines can be analog or digital, stand alone or linked with computers or copiers. They transmit all data on a page, including text, photos, illustrations, and so on. Fax machines are inexpensive and easy to operate. However, if signal transmission is interrupted, the receiver will not get the entire document as sent.

■ Document distribution involves using communicating word processors to transmit a document to any network user. Documents are exchanged by moving the document to the desired destination, by storing it in a host computer, or by a combination of the two. The heart of the system is generally a mail log maintained by electronic mail software.

■ Electronic message systems improve office productivity and facilitate communications by providing such functions as generalized documents and forms, distribution lists, reply, and search capabilities. Memos are created, stored, sent to electronic mailboxes, and retrieved by users.

■ Voicemail combines the answering machine with the functions of a computer. Users dial into the system and leave a voice message or memo in the recipient's voicemail box. The recipient then dials into the system to pick up messages.

■ Advantages of electronic message systems include: (a) they greatly reduce the time between creation of a message and its reception; (b) they overcome distance, time zones, and other delays; and (c) they increase worker productivity and facilitate internal communications.

■ Disadvantages include: (a) lack of standardized and compatible equipment and (b) "skewed use," that is, some employees use the system heavily while others hardly use it at all.

■ Guidelines for writing and filing memos in OAS systems are as follows: (a) read the memo and determine your response as soon as possible, (b) decide how to file the memo, (c) be able to retrieve the file, (d) conduct periodic house cleaning of files, and (e) back up important memos that should be saved.

■ Confidential memos should not be stored on shared media but delivered by hand or on secure floppy disks.

CHAPTER SEVEN

MODEL
MEMOS

▼

The model memos in this chapter are representative of the most common types of messages written in organizations. Some of the categories may overlap; for example, "Acknowledgment" and "Reply/Rejoinder" could be considered similar messages. We have resolved this problem by arranging memos according to the major emphasis of each message.

The model memos can be helpful in several ways. The guidelines given before each memo can help you to organize and write your own version of the required message. In other cases, you may be able to use roughly the same wording, and adapt the message to your own needs. Finally, the models may stimulate your own thoughts or emotions just enough to get your memo-writing process started. You may discover what you don't want to say as much as what you do need to cover.

This section can be useful to your secretary or assistant as well. If you need to delegate your memo-writing duties, this list should help the person find the proper category and wording for nearly all situations.

ACCOMPLISHMENTS, documenting. See also PROGRESS REPORTS. This memo is used to report on the success or achievement of an endeavor. If you have several accomplishments to report, list them in order of importance to the reader. Stick to the facts; don't exaggerate achievements to make them more dramatic. Be sure to point out those responsible for the achievement.

(Electronics manufacturer)

To: Richmond Desine, President
From: Morris Archer, Vice President Operations, Southeast
Date: February 12, 19—
Attachment: Rochelle Annual Report
Subject: SUCCESS OF NEW GEORGIA PLANT

I am happy to report that our new plant in Rochelle, Georgia, has been highly successful in its first two years of operation. I have attached the most recent annual report. The facts, in brief, are

■ Annual sales rose from 200,000 VCRs in the first year to more than 400,000 for the past year.

■ Profits realized in the second year exceeded $579,000, nearly $140,000 over projections.

■ The Rochelle plant's production output already rivals that of our other two Georgia plants in Gaston and Vale. Rochelle is currently producing 32,000 VCRs per month.

■ Increases in production costs at Rochelle averaged only 10 percent annually, among the lowest in the entire firm.

Credit for the success of the Rochelle plant goes to Vera Wales, Director, and her fine staff. I have every reason to believe they will continue their outstanding performance. I'll keep you informed. In the meantime, this crew deserves the "Division of the Year" award.

MA:ty
cc: Vera Wales, Director

ACKNOWLEDGMENT. See also REPLY/REJOINDER.
This type of memo is used to acknowledge someone's action or to let

them know you received material they sent. If you need to ask a question or make comments, do so after acknowledging the action or material received.

(Office supplies production plant)

To: Yvonne Atwater, Purchasing
From: Ivan Growski, Production Manager
Date: December 8, 19—
Reference: Parts Order 3345
Subject: Receipt of Component Parts

Our department has received the component parts we requested on November 3, 19—. Thank you for your prompt action.

However, my assistant discovered that three items are missing from the order: one platen knob, a printer head, and one antiglare screen. If these items are not in stock, please order them for our department.

IG:rs

ACTION, call for. See also COMPLAINTS; VIEWING WITH ALARM. In this message, you are pointing out a situation that needs to be corrected, providing a solution, and urging your readers to comply. Let readers know in the first paragraph what the problem is and why it needs immediate action. Be specific about what you want your readers to do, then close with an expression of appreciation for their cooperation. Keep a positive, optimistic tone that communicates confidence that they will comply.

(Corporate office building)

To: All Corporate Tenants
From: Sheila McCormick, Building Manager
Date: May 21, 19—
Subject: BUILDING SECURITY

We are asking everyone's cooperation in making Granfield Building a more secure place in which to work. In the past few weeks, several unauthorized people have entered the building's offices. Although no serious incidents have occurred, a few employees in the building have reported the theft of personal items.

The security guards do their best to ensure that only authorized people are allowed into the building. However, they must occasionally leave their stations.

We urge all occupants to keep a watchful eye out for strangers in the halls, in private offices, or in other locations in the building. Please challenge anyone you do not recognize and feel free to call the security guards at any sign of trouble. If we all work together, we can make Granfield Building a safe place for everyone.

SM:wd

ADVOCACY

At various times, you may want to state your views; support a cause; or argue for or against a policy, decision, or principle. Or someone may seek your point of view, judgment, or counsel on a particular matter. The tone of your memo should not be too strong or too weak. You don't want to appear too argumentative or too bland.

An effective advocacy memo contains:

■ A brief description of the situation
■ Statement of your recommendations
■ Reasons behind your recommendations

(Any large organization)

To: Ella Lebeau, Vice President
From: Bernard Loos, Director
Date: July 15, 19—
Subject: REDUCING BIMONTHLY MEETINGS

Although we generally accomplish a fair amount in our current bimonthly meetings, they take a great deal of time out of each manager's work day. By my calculations, the average meeting runs 2½ to 3 hours from start to finish. This does not count the time each manager spends completing a progress report to present at the meeting.

I suggest that we reduce the number of monthly assessment and planning meetings from two to one. If everyone knows we have only one meeting in which to conduct business, he/she will make a greater effort to be on time and have reports finished. As a result, I believe we can accomplish just as much work in a single meeting held once a month as we currently do in two meetings. Instead of attending a second meeting, the managers can use their time to conduct company business.

BL:op

AGREEMENT

Agreement memos generally fall into two categories: acquiescence or a statement of understanding. In the first, you are agreeing with a colleague or superior about a particular matter. In the second, you agree to do something with or for someone. The sample memo below illustrates agreement as acquiescence.

(Fast-food restaurant chain)

To: Noreen Walters, Director of Marketing
From: Herbert Calloway, Manager, Dan's Ranch House
Date: September 19, 19—
Subject: SOFT DRINK PROMOTIONAL CAMPAIGN

I wholeheartedly agree with your suggestion that we offer free soft drinks with all entrees $5.00 and over during the month of November. All the managers in this area are experiencing a drop in business since the Burritos chain moved in. This promotional campaign should get more customers back into our restaurants.

When it comes time to present the idea to headquarters, you can count on our support. Let me know what you want us to do.

HC:nb
cc: All area managers

ANNOUNCEMENTS

Announcements are among the most common memos circulated in companies. They inform employees about decisions made, actions taken, job changes, new hires, resignations, births, weddings, and a host of other topics. Accuracy in all details is paramount in such memos.

(Travel agency)

To: All Agency Staff
From: Veronica Presnell, Office Manager
Date: June 5, 19—
Subject: NEW CARPET FOR AGENCY OFFICE

Next weekend, June 13–14, we will be recarpeting the entire agency office. Therefore, before you leave work on Friday, please make sure all wastebaskets, chairs, boxes, and other items on the floors are moved into the hallway.

Also, clear your desk tops and either put your belongings in your desk drawers (which should be locked) or in boxes. Please label your boxes so that you can find your belongings easily Monday morning.

I'm sure we all appreciate getting the new carpeting. Our old carpet has definitely seen better days!

VP

APOLOGY

Occasionally, even the best people make mistakes, fail to keep their promises, or allow situations to get out of hand, and they need to apologize. Follow these tips to avoid sending an apology that aggravates rather than resolves a situation.

- Focus on the action taken, *not* on the damage done by your error. Tell the recipient what you have done to rectify the situation.
- Explain briefly how the mistake happened and apologize.
- Assure the reader that you value his or her goodwill.
- Tell the reader how you will guard against future mistakes.

(Any organization)

To: Candace Vorzinsky, Customer Service Representative
From: Inez Jacobs, Director of Accounting
Date: August 25, 19 —
Subject: CUSTOMER REFUNDS

I have corrected the computer programming error that has caused repeated delays in customer refunds over the past two months. Refunds can now be processed within three hours from the time we receive the paperwork from your department. This will eliminate any delay in issuing refund checks to customers.

The error was traced to a faulty programming command embedded in the system which made it difficult to correct. Please accept my apology for the inconvenience and distress this problem has caused you and your staff. I realize that your department has had to deal with a multitude of angry customers.

We have instituted new safeguards against such a programming error occurring again. I hope that with renewed cooperation and goodwill between our departments we can provide even better service to the customer.

IJ:edf
cc: Warren Tyson, Divisional Vice President

APPROVAL. See AUTHORIZATION.

ASSIGNMENT AND DELEGATION

An *assignment* is a task given by a manager to a subordinate that falls within the job responsibilities of the subordinate. *Delegation,* on the other hand, involves asking a subordinate to take over a task that is usually the manager's responsibility—such as running the department while the manager is on vacation.

In some cases, it's a wise idea to put the assignment or delegation in writing. Such a memo serves as instructions to a subordinate, and informs others who need to know that the employee has been given specific responsibilities.

(Book publisher)

To: All Copy Department Personnel
From: Sarah Dryden, Managing Editor
Date: October 9, 19—
Subject: Changes in Duties of Ann Carpenter and Bob Gidden

As we begin the busiest time of our editorial schedule, we will all be making greater demands on Ann Carpenter's time. To give her more time to deal directly with authors, I have decided to assign some of her duties to Bob Gidden.

From now until December 31, Bob will keep a dated record of each manuscript's progress through the copy department. He will track the manuscript from the time it leaves the author's hands, through all editorial and production stages, to final proofs. If you need to know the status of any manuscript, check with Bob.

Ann will continue to ensure that authors meet their deadlines and that they receive payment and final proofs. Direct all your questions about author correspondence to her.

These changes should not only streamline our workflow but help to conserve Ann's sanity through the hectic months ahead.

SD:dfg
cc: Personnel Department

AUTHORIZATION

An authorization memo is a written record that you have granted someone permission to do something—take a day off, order merchandise, investigate a prospective client, and so on. In additon to giving permission, you may also want to include any modifications, conditions, or limitations on what may be done.

Putting authorizations in writing can be a wise precaution. Should any question arise later about who authorized the action or what the authorization involved, your memo will serve as a source document.

(Electronics firm)

To: Gina Uleland, Payroll
From: Carlson Richards, Director, Research and Development
Date: February 18, 19—
Subject: TUITION REIMBURSEMENT FOR JOHN MALLORY

I hereby authorize the reimbursement to John Mallory of $350 tuition he paid to attend the class "Frontiers in Electronics Technology" at the University of Chicago. John forwarded the tuition reimbursement form to your department on January 15.

I assured him that because the class is directly related to his work here he would be reimbursed for the tuition expense. We both agreed, however, that his second class, "How to Use Your Personal Computer for Profit," does not qualify for reimbursement.

CR:jkl

BIDS, asking for

On occasion you may be required to solicit bids from companies for various equipment or supplies. The key to this message is accuracy and completeness of details: tell the readers precisely what you need, including illustrations or specifications whenever possible. Let them know when you need the bid, and give them a person to contact if they have any questions or require further information. Learning how to write effective bid memos can help to streamline the purchasing process.

(Food service manufacturer)

To: Henry Ridenhaur, Electrical Contractor
From: Marlene Towers, Purchasing Agent
Date: March 1, 19—
Attachments: Blueprints and floor plan
Subject: BID FOR ELECTRICAL WIRING OF WAREHOUSE ADDITION

We would like your bid on the electrical wiring of a new addition we are planning to our warehouse. The blueprints of the addition and floor plans for the intended placement of the freezers are attached.

We plan to install the following equipment:

- One walk-in freezer
- At least one bank of lights running the length of the freezer
- Three reach-in freezer chests, commercial grade

We also need to know whether a bank of lights or individual hanging lights would be most suitable for the addition. Send us specific details and a bid for the lighting configuration you would recommend.

Please submit your bid by March 31, 19—. Mail it to us, marked "Attn: Marlene Towers." If you have any questions, please call me at 347-7899.

MT:pkj

CLARIFICATION
This type of memo can be used either to ask for clarification or to give clarification regarding an issue, situation, or event. In both cases, the memo must be crystal clear.

If you are asking for clarification, be specific about what you want to know. If you are explaining, make sure you use lists, headings, or other devices to help you get your point across. A message meant to end confusion should not end up confusing the situation even more.

(Banking institution)

To: All Tellers and Accounting Employees
From: Sharon L. Periwhite, General Bank Manager
Date: June 3, 19—
Attachments: Form letters
Subject: CHECK CLEARANCE POLICY

In my memo of April 15, I explained that beginning August 1 our checks will no longer clear through First National Bank of Wilmington. Instead, they will clear through People's Trust of Starkville. We notified our checking account customers of this fact in May and supplied each one with 100 new checks free of charge.

However, there seems to be some confusion among our staff about our policy for honoring checks written or received after the August 1 date. The policy is as follows:

1. *Any check dated August 1 or later will NOT be honored.*
As a courtesy, we informed customers of the change two months in advance. Therefore, any check dated August 1 or later should be returned to the customer with an explanatory letter (see Number 1 form letter attached). A $5.00 processing fee will be debited from the customer's account.

Customer complaints arising from this policy should be handled firmly but diplomatically. If any case seems unclear or exceptional, please refer the customer to me. I am the only person authorized to grant exceptions to this policy.

2. *Checks dated before August 1 but received after that date WILL be honored provided they are received DURING THE MONTH OF AUGUST.* This grace period will allow a reasonable time for the payee to process such checks.

3. *Checks dated before August 1 but received by us on or after September 1 will NOT be honored.* These checks should be returned to the customer with an explanatory letter (see Number 2 form letter attached). Customers will NOT be charged a fee, however, because they are not responsible for the payee's delay in processing the check.

Please be sure you understand this policy clearly. A courteous, well-informed staff can help to make the transition in operations easier for customers and bank personnel alike. Your cooperation in this matter is greatly appreciated.

SLP:rs
cc: Division Vice President

COMMENDATION. See also ACCOMPLISHMENTS.

This memo is one of the more pleasant messages to write. You are acknowledging the good work of a subordinate and encouraging the person to keep it up. In writing the memo, state specifically what action or suggestion you appreciated and what results it has had. Such memos can motivate other employees. You may wish to have a copy of the message placed in the person's file.

(Medical testing lab)

To: Julie Mamchur, Laboratory Assistant
From: Oliver Eccles, Director
Date: June 17, 19—
Subject: Your Money-Saving Suggestion

Your suggestion of an alternative supplier for our laboratory glassware is an excellent one. Quite frankly, we'd be foolish not to switch suppliers. I anticipate the change will save us several thousand dollars over the next year or two.

It's good to know that my laboratory staff has good business sense as well as medical expertise. With the savings in glassware, I think we can manage that new autoclave you wanted. Keep up the good work — and keep those ideas coming!

OE:sf

cc: Personnel files

COMPLAINTS. See also ACTION, call for; PROTESTS; VIEWING WITH ALARM.

In no memo is tone so important as in a complaint message. You don't want to attack the recipients or make excuses for them. Your purpose is to state the problem and to find a satisfactory solution, if possible. A combination of functional and problem—solution sequences is the best format to follow.

To ensure the best chances of success:

■ Let the reader know your exact complaint. Give enough detail so that the person knows the situation. Don't dwell on how much grief it has caused you. Where appropriate, give specific names or dates and any copies of past correspondence on the subject for the reader's convenience.

■ Suggest the action or solution you want, but be open to negotiation. If you have no solutions, ask your reader for suggestions.

■ Keep the tone positive and conciliatory. Don't assume the mistake is intentional; give people the benefit of the doubt even if that means saving the other person's face a little. They will be far more likely to come up with an adequate solution.

(Any postal station)

To: Howard Concord, Mail carrier
From: Dan Arguiles, Postal clerk
Date: January 9, 19—
Subject: MAIL HOLDS

In the past month I've received numerous complaints from local patrons on your Dodson area route about mail holds. Patrons state they sometimes receive mail during the hold period or don't receive mail after delivery should have been resumed. Naturally, they are unhappy with our service.

Please read all mail-hold requests carefully and double-check the dates to make sure when to stop and resume service. On my end, I will make sure that customers fill out both stopping and starting dates.

If we work together on this, it will make both our jobs easier and the patrons a lot happier.

DA

CONDOLENCES

Expressions of sympathy can be a welcome touch to someone in the firm who has had a setback, major illness, or death in the family. Although such messages may be written as letters instead of memos, we include them here as a key area of intracompany communication. What you choose to say depends on your relationship with the recipient and your actual feelings. A general rule of thumb is to keep the message simple: acknowledge the person's loss, speak of your own feelings, and offer your sympathy and/or help.

(Any organization)

To: Dale Good
From: Arleen Speck, President
Date: November 12, 19—
Subject: CONDOLENCE

I was deeply saddened to hear of your wife's passing last week. I remember her fondly from various corporate functions where we met, and I know she will be greatly missed. She was a kind, warm person with a keen wit, and we always looked forward to her company. Please accept my deepest sympathy for your tragic loss.

AS:trk

CONFIRMATION

This type of memo is among the most important you will write. It provides a written, often detailed record of arrangements or agreements made verbally. Confirmation can refer to a past, present, or future event.

■ Use the functional sequence in writing confirmations.
■ Put down all details of the arrangement or agreement: dates, names, places, amounts, tasks, and so on.
■ Mention the date of any initial personal, phone, or written agreements, contracts, requests, or meetings.
■ Ask the reader to correct any errors in the content of your memo and provide a telephone number or address where you can be contacted.

(Any organization)

To: Jean O'Mara, Supervisor
From: Donna Bell, Assistant
Date: May 22, 19—
Subject: VACATION—June 3-10

This is to confirm our conversation of this morning concerning the dates of my vacation and arrangements in my absence. I will be out of town for a week beginning Monday, June 3, and will return to the office on Monday, June 10.

During my absence, I've arranged for a temporary secretary, Mary Pearson, to handle my duties. I've already "shown her the ropes," and she knows what her responsibilities will be.

If you need to contact me during the week of June 3-10, I can be reached at (414) 432-6289. Mary also has the address and telephone number of the hotel where I will be staying. I'll think of you all while I'm in San Francisco.

DB

CONGRATULATIONS

Like commendations, congratulatory memos recognize an individual's or group's achievement, award, or special status. Be specific in your praise, mentioning the achievement and qualities you recognize and admire in the person. Don't overdo your praise, however, particularly to a superior in the firm. You want to be regarded as sincere in your congratulations, not as a flatterer.

(Any organization)

To: Nadine Gorman, Vice President
From: Hanley Kyle, Director
Date: June 19, 19—
Subject: "Executive of the Year" Award

Congratulations on winning the Chamber of Commerce's "Executive of the Year" award. It's a fine tribute to your leadership in the company and to your work in the city's community colleges.

Since you joined the firm, I know the company has made great strides in recovering from severe financial setbacks. How you managed that feat while fitting in so many hours of charity work is beyond me, but you have my sincere admiration.

Congratulations again. Your award is richly deserved.

HK:afd

COVERING MEMO. See also **TRANSMITTAL.**
This message has one point to make: to record the transmittal of material ("Enclosed is a copy of the Johnson report you requested. . ."). In some cases, you may want to comment on the material, summarize important points, or point out the conditions under which the material is loaned.

(Any hospital)

To: Department Laboratory Technicians
From: Ruby Glacias, Chief Technician
Date: June 7, 19—
Attachment: Ultrasound Plus Operations Manual
Subject: NEW ULTRASOUND EQUIPMENT MANUAL

Attached is a copy of the operations manual for the ultrasound equipment we received last week. Please read it carefully and write down any questions you have.

Next Tuesday, June 10, from 8 am to 4 pm we will have our first training session using the new equipment. The manufacturer's training staff will answer all your questions at that time. If you need additional copies of the manual, please see Fred Krause in Purchasing.

RG:ibn

CRITICISM/REPRIMAND

Effective criticism is an important part of management and supervision. Messages that "put down" the recipient, however, can make the situation worse. To write effective criticism follow these guidelines:

■ Keep a positive tone. You are not out to berate the person or to cut him or her down with sarcasm or scorn.

■ Criticize the act and not the person. Instead of dwelling on the character of your recipient, state clearly what the problem is and what needs to be changed.

■ Emphasize "I statements" over "you statements." Rather than say "You have failed to turn in your department records on time again" tell the person, "I understand your department records were late again."

■ Express confidence that the situation can be changed. State what results you want and solicit the recipient's ideas and cooperation.

■ When necessary, usually by the second warning, state the consequences if the recipient fails to resolve the situation.

(Industrial chemical manufacturing plant)

To: Austin Nunn, Plant Manager
From: Gregory Appleton, Division Manager
Date: August 14, 19—
Subject: TOXIC LEAKS FROM CONTAINMENT DRUMS

Last month I received notice from the local EPA inspector that our containment drums were leaking toxic chemicals during shipment. I mentioned the notice to you, and you assured me that the problem would be corrected.

Today I received a second warning from the EPA. They found chemicals leaking from a recent shipment. I find it disturbing that this problem has not been corrected. It is not only a financial loss to ourselves and our customers but also we could be assessed a heavy fine by the EPA for allowing hazardous chemicals to leak into the environment.

Austin, I can't stress enough the seriousness of this problem and the need for immediate action. Please conduct an investigation and prepare a report on the cause and solution of the chemical leaks. I respect your expertise in chemical manufacturing and your long record with the plant. I am sure you will be able to handle this problem and prevent any further citations from the EPA.

Next week I'll make a trip to the plant, and we can discuss what needs to be done.

GA:svn

DISAGREEMENT

Although you don't always need to put your contrary opinion in writing, a written statement is appropriate when

- Someone has asked for your opinion.
- You want to put your views on record.
- Your disagreement can be constructive.

When stating your contrary opinion, keep your emotions under control. This is not the time to blast someone else's ideas or to give the impression you are a sore loser. State your case clearly and concisely, backing it up with facts, then leave the reader free to decide whether to act on your opinion.

(Nonprofit organization)

To: Jerry Pruit, Fund-raising Chairman
From: Karl Wade, Committee Member

Date: September 30, 19—

Subject: DIRECT MAIL CAMPAIGN

Jerry, your suggestion to push ahead with a direct mail campaign to solicit donations is an excellent one. I agree with all your points except one: the strategy to start mailing requests in January of next year.

According to fund-raising experts, January is an excellent month for soliciting publication subscriptions but a poor one for soliciting charitable contributions. No one has been able to explain this paradox in consumer behavior. The best months for charitable contributions remain November and December, when the holidays put people in a giving mood.

I strongly recommend we initiate our direct mail campaign in November and December. I realize we will be competing with a lot of other organizations, but I think our promotional materials are superior to most. If this idea doesn't appeal to you, how about starting the campaign a little later in the new year? People will have time to recuperate financially, and they may be in a more giving mood by Easter.

Please give the matter some thought. Whatever you decide, I will be supportive in any way I can.

KW

DISMISSALS

You may have occasion to write one of three types of dismissal memos

■ Describing to a third party (personnel, management, etc.) why an employee is being dismissed. These memos document the facts and serve as a record of action taken.

■ Telling employees they are let go through no fault of their own—plant closings, financial reverses, failing business, etc.

■ Telling employees they are fired for violations of company rules, poor work performance, or some other action on the individual's part.

Use the functional sequence in writing the first type of dismissal memo. For the others, use the diamond sequence. Give the reasons for termination, being as truthful, objective, and clear as possible before announcing the dismissal.

Word the memo as positively as you can, but don't gloss over the facts merely to spare the employee's ego. If you are too ambiguous about the reasons for dismissal, such statements may be used against you if the employee later challenges your decision. Always make sure that documented reasons are listed in file memos.

(Manufacturing plant)

To: Richard Carlisle, Product Engineer
From: Pauline Fredericks, Division Manager
Date: April 23, 19 —
Subject: [Leave subject line blank]

Over the past six months your supervisor and I have worked with you regarding your difficulties in finishing assignments on time. Recently, however, the failure to meet deadlines resulted in the loss of two critical government contracts. We feel that although you have the necessary technical skill, your work style is not compatible with our company's requirements.

Therefore, it is with considerable regret that we must terminate your employment contract, effective Friday, April 25. Attached is an outline of your termination benefits and conversion options regarding company pension, insurance, and profit-sharing plans. Your medical insurance will be extended for six months, and you will receive two months' severance pay.

We would also like to assist you in your search for a new position. Please contact Wilma Hite in Human Resources for an appointment to discuss your situation.

I sincerely regret having to take this step. Be assured, however, that our policy on giving references is to release only employment dates and job titles. You are a talented engineer, and we wish you every success in your future employment.

PF:tns

Attachments

ENCOURAGEMENT

Like the congratulations or commendation memo, a message of encouragement can be an effective motivator. It tells the reader that you value not only *what* is happening but *who* is responsible. Recognition of good work is one of the most basic needs of employees, regardless of rank.

(Any organization)

To: Sales Staff

From: Michelle Perringer, Manager of Sales

Date: March 6, 19 —

Subject: QUARTERLY SALES FIGURES

I've just seen the sales figures for the first quarter, and I'm happy to announce we're ahead of last year's figure by 20 percent! This great performance reflects the dedication and hard work of the entire sales staff. Let's see if we can continue the good work and beat last year's record for the remaining three quarters.

MP:wrt

FAREWELL

Farewells are in order for a resignation, retirement, transfer, promotion, or any other situation in which an employee is leaving your department or the company. The nature of your relationship and the circumstances of the departure will determine what you say in your memo.

Be sincere, informal, and personal without getting overly sentimental or flowery. This memo is a good opportunity to comment on the individual's personal traits you admired, his or her contribution to the company, and any future plans.

(Any organization)

To: Beatrice Newton
From: Evelyn Shofield
Date: September 11, 19—
Subject: Saying Goodbye

I heard from Alan that you'll be leaving the company at the end of the month and moving to Minneapolis. I'll certainly miss you and the great times we had getting all those mailings out the door.

During these past four years, it's been a pleasure to work with you. I've never known you to turn down any job, no matter how big or how small. No deadline was ever too tight, and no joke was ever too corny to make you laugh.

I wish you the best of luck in your new position and hope you've got plenty of sweaters for those long Minnesota nights. Drop us a line now and then and let us know how you're doing!

ES

FOLLOW-UP

Follow-up memos are written for two purposes:

■ A previous message or action has not produced the desired response or results.

■ A previous message or action requires further comment.

To get the best results from your follow-up memo, make sure you restate your original message or request for action. Don't rely on previous correspondence that may have gotten lost, mislaid, or destroyed. Offer an explanation for your reader's failure to comply—allowing for a little face saving on the reader's part. Stress the need for a response. If appropriate, state when you expect to hear from her/him and what your next step will be if you don't receive a reply.

(Construction company)

To: Norm Cancilleri, Contractor
From: Jason Neubard, Construction Site Superintendent
Date: November 3, 19—
Subject: COPPER TUBING FOR FEDERATED LIFE BUILDING

Norm, as I mentioned in my October 25 memo, we need another order of copper tubing if we are to complete construction of the Federated Life Insurance Building on time. As of this week, we still have not received the order.

Could you look into this matter? If I don't hear from you by tomorrow, I'll be forced to lay off half my crew, which will cost us several thousand dollars. We can't do any more work on the sixth floor until we get the tubing. Let me know when we can expect the order.

JN:dsf

GRATITUDE

Recognition and appreciation are two of the most sought after yet rarely given rewards in corporate life. Make it a point to express your gratitude whenever you have the chance. Avoid being effusive or too abrupt in your memos. Keep two questions in mind as you write:

■ How do you feel about what has been done? (How has it touched you personally?)
■ Why are you grateful? (What is it that you are able to do as a result of someone's help or good work?)

(Newspaper)

To: Jacqueline Valasquez, Staff Photographer
From: Carol Fisher, Staff Reporter

Date: May 21, 19—

Subject: ROCKY MOUNTAIN AIRLINES CRASH STORY

As you've probably heard, the managing editor loved the spread we did on the Rocky Mountain Airlines crash. Too often the reporter gets most of the credit for a story like that.

I just wanted to tell you that in my five years with the paper, I've never appreciated anyone's professional support more than I did yours that afternoon. Without your photos, my words wouldn't have had half their power. You got some hard-hitting shots that made all the difference in the way the piece affected the reader. Thanks for your help!

CF

HIRING

How you introduce a newly hired employee to the company can have considerable impact on the way the individual is perceived by others. For this reason, a "new hire" memo deserves separate treatment from the more traditional announcement memos.

Strike a balance in your introduction between praise and understatement. If you are too glowing and laudatory — particularly about someone entering the upper management ranks — expectations from colleagues may be set too high. On the other hand, the new executive's peers may feel threatened and decide in advance to isolate their newest member. When in doubt, lean in favor of the more subtle approach.

Most "new hire" memos, however, will be straightforward presentations of the individual's qualifications and responsibilities.

(Art museum)

To: All Staff Members
From: Gloria LeBoult, Museum Director
Date: October 12, 19—
Subject: JOHN SAMUELSON, CURATOR

It is my pleasure to announce that, effective October 15, John Samuelson will assume the responsibilities of Curator at Hamilton

Museum. For the past ten years, John has been in charge of nineteenth-century American art acquisitions at the Philadelphia Museum of Art. Under his able guidance, the museum has acquired an outstanding collection of American frontier artwork.

John received his early training at the Pennsylvania Academy of Fine Arts. He has been granted honorary degrees from the University of Chicago and Brown University. Over the past two years, John has served as advisor in American art to both the Tate Gallery and the Victoria and Albert Museum in London.

We are fortunate to obtain such a highly qualified, dedicated curator. Please join me in welcoming a valuable new colleague to our staff.

GL:kyl

IDEAS
The category of ideas also includes suggestions and proposals. You may have several reasons for communicating ideas:

■ For the record—you want your idea in writing to document the date and details.
■ "For Your Information"—an FYI memo alerts someone to an idea you feel they might be able to use.
■ For further development—your idea may be incomplete and you want someone else to help you develop it.

You may want to use a functional or problem—solution sequence to describe your idea. If you want to persuade or sell someone on a suggestion, make sure you have given them sufficient detail to judge the merits of your proposal.

(Any large organization)

To: Constance Black, President/CEO
From: Karen Horton, Company Nurse

Date: February 4, 19—
Subject: AEROBICS CLASS FOR EMPLOYEES

I believe I have a solution to a chronic midwinter problem. Each year at this time, I see a large number of employees suffering from various health complaints and bouts of depression. The truth is these "midwinter blues" have a physical cause. In cold weather people tend to exercise less, which affects their physical and mental health.

I suggest that we offer an employee aerobics class two to three nights a week in the company cafeteria for the next two months. Employees could be charged a nominal fee to cover the cost of hiring a local aerobics instructor. We could encourage employees to sign up for the class by pointing out the health benefits and the convenience of having the class at work.

Aerobics courses have been very successful at other companies. I'm sure a course in our firm would improve employee health, morale, and productivity, and perhaps even help us to cut back on company medical insurance costs. If this idea appeals to you, I'd be happy to discuss it further at your convenience.

KH

INQUIRY

An inquiry memo is generally a brief message that raises a question and asks for a reply. This simple-sounding memo is a vital communications link in any company. It can prevent unnecessary work (should a project be initiated?) and supply missing information needed to resolve a problem (what is the discount price on volume purchases?).

(Mail order company)

To: Yuri Cross, Director of Merchandising
From: Shanna Hirshfield, Director, Customer Order Department

Date: March 4, 19—

Subject: PRICE OF LEAF SHREDDER

Yuri, I've come across a discrepancy in the price of our leaf shredder (K431-0916) listed in our spring catalog. Our department records show the price as $125.99 plus tax and shipping. The catalog lists the price as $115.99 plus tax and shipping.

Which is the correct price? Please let me know as soon as possible.

SH:trj

INSPECTION

If you are asked to inspect property, machinery, or other items, follow these guidelines when you write your memo:

- State your general evaluation first ("sound with minor exceptions...," "serious problems with...," "no major flaws...").
- List specific findings in a way that is easiest for the reader to follow (order of importance, by physical layout, from most to least expensive, etc.).
- If necessary, explain why each problem developed.
- State your recommendations or what action should be taken to correct the problems. Include specific time and cost estimates if you can obtain the information.
- Attach any illustrative material to help the reader understand the problems.

(Real estate firm)

To: Julia R. Seabury, President, Cypress Realty

From: Paul McHinery, Real Estate Inspector

Date: January 29, 19—

Subject: COMMERCIAL INSPECTION AT 2121 CENTRAL

At your request, I inspected the commercial property at 2121 Central on January 27, 19—. Based on my initial inspection, the property is structurally sound, but in need of extensive plumbing and electrical repairs. In addition, four of the interior walls and part of the flooring show considerable water damage from leaking pipes.

All the problems I found are typical of buildings that are 50 years old or older, such as this one is. The property is simply showing its age and needs to be renovated. Specific problems and recommendations are as follows:

- *Electrical wiring* — This is the most serious problem. My initial tests indicate there is a short somewhere in the system. If any office equipment or other machinery were plugged into the outlets, the short could cause an electrical fire. I recommend we call in an electrical contractor to get an estimate on rewiring the building.
- *Plumbing* — Plumbing in all three washrooms needs to be replaced completely. I recommend contacting Younger & Coles for the work; they specialize in refitting older buildings.
- *Interior wall and flooring* — Water-damaged walls and flooring will need to be repaired or replaced. Any of several contractors can do this work. I think we've used Younger & Coles for such jobs in the past.

The cost for rehabbing the building should run between $25,000 and $35,000. I believe the property's value justifies the expense. It is basically sound and located on a prime commercial corner. In today's market we should realize a profit of $250,000 on its sale.

If you have any questions, please contact me at 455-6700.

PM:ddf

INTRODUCTION

These memos are used to introduce a new product, equipment, service, form, or other new item that is coming out immediately. When you write your memo, include the word "new" or an equivalent term in the subject heading to call attention to the item. Explain how the product, service, equipment, or form works and what its advantages are. Be sure to mention any limitations or exceptions that apply. Mention how readers can find out more about the item or who can answer their questions.

(Import/export distribution company)

To: All Import/Export Executives
From: Tricia Caldwell, Finance and Accounting
Date: July 8, 19—
Subject: NEW FREQUENT-FLYER CREDIT CARDS

The company is introducing a new frequent-flyer credit card called WORLDWIDE VISA for use on any business-related flights on United or American Airlines. You will receive your card and a brochure outlining the terms and conditions of the program by July 16. Some of the highlights of the program include:

- WORLDWIDE VISA guarantees you first-class accommodations even with business or coach fares.
- You need accumulate only 10,000 miles before you are eligible for your first free trip for you and another person anywhere in the Western Hemisphere.
- WORLDWIDE VISA entitles you to a 50 percent discount on all hotel and motel reservations and guarantees you a second night free if you are forced to layover.
- WORLDWIDE VISA offers a 30 percent discount on all car rentals with free, unlimited mileage.

Use of the card is limited to *employees only*. Family members are not eligible to participate in the program nor can the card be used for personal airline trips, hotel reservations, or car rentals. The company will assume all membership fees associated with the credit card, and accounting will verify all charges made. Any cards reported lost or stolen will be replaced within 24 hours.

We encourage you to use WORLDWIDE VISA whenever you travel on company business. The new card should help us cut travel expenses and obtain better service in major cities around the world.

When you receive the WORLDWIDE VISA brochure, please read it carefully. If you have any questions about the card or about company policy, contact Estelle Richards at ex. 305.

TC:gh

INVITATIONS

Invitation memos should name the event or occasion in the first sentence. The memos must include all details regarding dates, times, places, cost, attire, reservations required, travel directions, contact name, and so on. If you are inviting someone to speak at a function, include an outline of the topic and ask if they have any special needs (equipment, transportation, visual aids, etc.). If appropriate, describe the agenda of the function, because many people will decide to attend solely on the basis of the program.

(Any corporation)

To: All Employees
From: Desmond Booth, President/CEO
Date: December 10, 19—
Subject: ANNUAL CHRISTMAS PARTY

You and a guest are invited to the company's annual Christmas party to be held Friday, December 23, beginning at 5:30 PM. In recognition of the company's success this past year, we are celebrating in style. The Christmas party will be held in the ballroom of the downtown Marriott Hotel, 275 W. Warren.

The party promises to be a gala affair. We have engaged a ballroom orchestra for the occasion, and plenty of free refreshments will be on hand. The cash bar will be open from 5:30 to 8:00.

I hope everyone will be able to join the celebration. You have all contributed to our success, and you all deserve to celebrate. Please

R.S.V.P. to Pat Conroy in Personnel by Friday, December 15. I look forward to seeing you there.

DB:hsd

JOB DESCRIPTIONS
Job descriptions are an important tool in finding the right person to fill a vacancy. The following guidelines can help you to write a concise, effective job description:

■ Introduce the description with a statement of overall responsibilities.
■ State to whom the employees reports.
■ List specific qualifications required to perform the job.
■ List responsibilities of the job, stating them in terms of actions that can be performed and measured. ("Develops and submits all budget estimates quarterly.")
■ Where appropriate, list sources of information needed to perform the job.

Use headings and lists to arrange information on the page and keep your wording brief, as in a resume.

(Municipal public transit office)

To: Personnel Department
From: Thomas White, Transit Supervisor
Date: March 27, 19—
Subject: JOB DESCRIPTION—MUNICIPAL TRANSIT AUTHORITY OPERATOR

Position: Municipal Transit Operator

Reports to: Transit Supervisor

Summary: The municipal transit operator is responsible for transporting the public safely on a municipal bus. Route and schedule are determined by the director of transit operations.

Qualifications:

- At least 21 years of age
- Valid state driver's license
- Good driving record
- In excellent health — 20/20 corrected vision
- Successful completion of 21-day drivers' training course.

Responsibilities:

- Drive diesel-powered bus along designated route and on time schedule established by director of transit operations
- Report any breakdowns or faulty machinery on the bus to transit supervisor
- Operate fare machines and distribute transfers
- Transport passengers safely and courteously
- Attend regular driver-training sessions

TW:rj

MEETINGS, agenda for

In general, when you announce a meeting, include the agenda. Be specific about the topics to be discussed. Such specificity lets readers know what the meeting will cover and gives them a chance to collect any materials they may need to bring. If necessary, ask for confirmation of attendance; if key people cannot make the meeting, you can reschedule. Give any premeeting assignments along with your memo so that attendees can arrive prepared.

(Any college or university)

To: All Officers of Alumni Association
From: Frieda Weeds, President of Alumni Association
Date: June 10, 19 —
Subject: JUNE 15 MEETING

The following items are on the agenda for our meeting on Friday, June 15, at 2:00 PM in the staff lounge:

■ Fund-raising campaign. We need to select an organizer, form a committee, and decide on a schedule for the campaign.

■ Welcoming Bob Watkins, the new football coach. Bob will be arriving on campus within two weeks and we need to plan a proper reception for him. He's going to have a tough job ahead of him turning our athletic program around.

■ Following up on our alumni. We need to gather more information about our alumni and find ways to make their activities known to other alums. This issue has been mentioned by several of our alumni.

If you have other agenda items, please pass them on to me by Wednesday, June 13. We have a lot of work to do at this meeting, so be sure to arrive on time.

FW:vgh

MEETINGS, recap of

Memos recapping a meeting clarify for the attendees, and others who are interested, exactly what occurred: decisions made, votes taken, topics rejected or tabled, disagreements, and so on. Items can be listed either in the order in which they were discussed or in order of importance. Double-check your facts before you send out your memo. It may be the only written record of the meeting and as such could be an important reference source at a later date.

To: All Officers of the Alumni Association
From: Frieda Weeds, President
Date: June 16, 19 —
Subject: RECAP OF JUNE 15 MEETING

We accomplished quite a bit in our June 15 meeting, setting our Association's priorities for the next few months. Here is a recap of the projects we voted to undertake this year.

■ *Mail campaign for the Meisner Fine Arts Building* — In July we will launch a direct-mail campaign to all alumni to raise funds for the new fine arts building. In August, we will follow up the mailing with personal phone calls to alumni who have not contributed to the fund.

Judy Biss will coordinate this campaign and will hold an organizational meeting on June 20. Volunteers can contact Judy at 443-0712.

■ *Dinner welcoming new football coach* — The Association will host a dinner to welcome Bob Watkins, our new football coach, on August 23. We will make a special effort to round up former football players for the "Reunion Rally" before the dinner. Jean Harper will be in charge of all arrangements.

■ *New committee to follow up on alumni* — John Robard has agreed to form a new committee to gather information about the current activities of all alumni. John will select two or three alumni to be highlighted in each issue of our alumni newsletter.

We have a lot of exciting projects ahead of us, so let's all work together to make this our best year yet.

FW:ebg

NEGOTIATIONS

Although face-to-face discussions are generally the best way to settle ongoing issues, occasionally you will need to put your questions or comments in writing. Explain the issue under consideration and ask specific questions of your reader or state your comments briefly. Your memo is meant to provoke discussion and will probably lead to face-to-face talks.

(Any large corporation)

To: Vivian Court, Company Recruiter
From: Kathy Egan, Manager, Employee Benefits
Date: August 17, 19—
Subject: EVALUATION OF EMPLOYEE HEALTH BENEFITS

As T. C. Williams probably told you, we are hiring a cost-management firm to help us find ways to control employee health-care costs. Mr. Williams suggested to me that we should work together on evaluating what effects various cutbacks in benefits might have on corporate recruiting. I think his suggestion makes sense, because you know what benefits will help us to attract the best job candidates.

We can create several types of benefit packages, but deciding on the best package is difficult. Should we cut back on our coverage for outpatient services? Should we re-evaluate coverage for spouses and dependents? Can we increase employee contributions to medical plans?

I'd like to hear your ideas on these and other topics. Can we meet this Friday at 10:00 AM to discuss the possibilities?

KE:lsb

OBJECTIVES

There are several advantages to putting objectives in writing. Everyone understands the goals he/she is striving to achieve, what needs to be done to achieve them, and how to recognize when objectives have been met. Setting objectives is an important management function. When you write your memo, consider the following guidelines:

■ State objectives in terms of measurable goals — sales reached, number of clients contacted, appointments made, and so on.
■ Use precise language — if you review something, what do you plan to look for? If you want to improve something, to what extent?
■ Use headings and/or listings to itemize your objectives. Rank them in order of importance or by dates to be accomplished. If there is only one objective, break it down into smaller steps.

(Agricultural biotechnology company)

To: All Managers
From: Charles Kiley, President

Date: November 21, 19—

Subject: OBTAINING GOVERNMENT PERMIT FOR PLANT VACCINE

Our priority for the company this year is to obtain a government permit to field-test our new plant vaccine. To achieve this goal, we must accomplish the following objectives over the next ten months:

1. By January, hire a consultant with ties to the EPA. This individual will act as liaison between our company and the EPA and help us to satisfy EPA requirements for introducing genetically engineered biologic material into the field.

2. Collect all our research data and write up the results in a comprehensive report in support of our application for a testing permit. In order to complete the report by March, all laboratory testing and clinical logs need to be up to date by January.

3. Set up an advisory panel of expert witnesses who can be called upon to testify on behalf of our application for a permit. The panel should be composed of at least ten experts from various universities and major research facilities. The panel should be in place by March.

4. With the consultant, devise a public relations strategy for allaying public fears about plant vaccine use. We will need to create public relations materials—brochures, videos, speeches, etc.—to present to environmental groups and the media. Rory Cullough assures me the materials can be ready by January.

Field testing is the first step toward FDA approval and licensing of our plant vaccines. I am sure you are all aware what that could mean to our firm in terms of commercial sales. With all of us pitching in, I'm sure we can win that government permit.

CK:fsh

ORDERS AND INSTRUCTIONS
Although most orders and instructions are given verbally, in some instances it's a good idea to put them in writing. This is particularly true

when the task is complicated; when there is a change in policy or procedure; or when you need illustrations, forms, or other graphic materials to show employees how to do something.

Technically, orders are commands to do something while instructions tell someone what, when, where, how, and sometimes why something is to be done. Whether you write an order or instructions, the content of the message is the same: something needs to be done and the reader is the one to do it.

(Biotechnology firm)

To: Research and Development Staff
From: Nora Zefflen, Manager, Research and Development
Date: February 16, 19—
Attachment: Sample RDT time log
Subject: COMPUTER TIME-RECORDING SYSTEM

Beginning March 1 all staff members will record time spent on various projects via a computer logging system. This system will help us keep track of how much time is spent on which projects for future budget considerations. Record your time as follows:

1. Note time spent on each project in your current time log as you have always done.

2. When you are ready to record your time on computer, enter the code RDT plus your personal access number, then press ENTER.

3. When the RDT time log appears on the screen, consult your project codes list to find the proper job code. Enter the code plus the number of hours spent on the project to the nearest quarter hour. Press ENTER.

4. You may enter your time throughout the day, at the end of the day, or at the end of the week. Whichever method you choose, make sure you track your activities accurately.

5. When you have entered the final project time at the end of the day, or at the end of the week, press RECORD.

I have attached a sample completed RDT time log to show you what the computer file looks like. If you have any questions about these procedures, contact Bob Holtz in Information Management.

I realize this is one more task to do in an already full workday, but please make the extra effort. The additional data will make it much easier for us to evaluate which projects justify the time and money spent on them.

NZ:bn

ORIENTATION/WELCOME

New employees usually receive orientation information about the company in the form of brochures, insurance papers, annual reports, and other company materials. An orientation memo can be used as a cover letter introducing these materials or as a means of easing the new employee into unfamiliar surroundings and responsibilities. In the memo you can offer a welcoming hand, tips on how to handle the job, who to turn to for advice and counsel, and what to avoid.

(Investment brokerage firm)

To: Irene Fraser, Financial Consultant
From: Robert Isingale, Stockbroker
Date: July 15, 19 —
Subject: WELCOME TO LESCHER & BROWN

Just a note to say welcome to the firm! Tim Unger mentioned that your specialty is mutual funds, which fills a gap in our team. I'm confident you'll be a valuable addition to our consulting group, and I look forward to working with you.

One word of advice: Don't wait until 4:30 to log in all your calls. Everyone is checking out around that time and you may have to wait up to half an hour to access the sign-off program. If you have any trouble with your terminal or mastering our computer system, see

Frances Dodge. She is not only a computer wizard but one of the most generous people in the company.

As you may know, our firm has a reputation for providing the best financial services in the city. We're all proud of that reputation, and I hope you'll be proud to represent us. Best wishes for a fulfilling career at Lescher & Brown.

RI

PERFORMANCE APPRAISAL

Most managers dislike writing performance appraisals, particularly when they must report poor performances. There are definite guidelines, however, that can make the job easier and help you to avoid some common pitfalls.

- Summarize the employee's overall performance.
- Follow up with specific strengths and weaknesses. Don't use the "sandwich" technique, putting a strength between two weaknesses or vice versa. All strengths and weaknesses should get maximum attention. Try to state weaknesses in a positive way — "improvements needed" or "areas that need strengthening."
- Decide on the status of the employee and his or her progress. Do you recommend promotion, reassignment, further training, demotion, probation? Is the employee performing at the expected level or above or below it? Is there potential for advancement?
- Focus on characteristics that are appropriate to the employee's actual job duties. For example, don't dwell on math ability if the job calls primarily for interpersonal skills.
- Base your evaluation on total job effectiveness rather than on isolated situations that may stand out in your mind.
- Suggest ways to overcome weaknesses and build on strengths and provide follow-up measures — another appraisal in six months, for example.

(Manufacturing company)

To: Eugene Stegger, Manager

From: Kris Baker, Shop Supervisor

Date: May 7, 19—

Subject: PERFORMANCE APPRAISAL FOR JOHN MCKEENE

During the present six-months' review period, John McKeene's work as a machine operator has been fully satisfactory. He is a conscientious and reliable employee and has met all quotas set for the period. With attention to the developmental needs listed below, he will become an excellent operator. I recommend that he be given the standard 10 percent salary raise beginning in June.

Strengths

■ *Excellent ability to handle computerized machinery and to learn new equipment*: John has been a fast learner. He handles all computerized machinery with considerable skill and care and shows above-average attention to the maintenance schedules for equipment.

■ *Excellent ability to understand and carry out job assignments*: He is quick to grasp what is required of each job and is able to deliver machined parts to exact specifications. His attention to product quality is outstanding.

■ *Good relationships with co-workers*: John is well liked by the other men in the shop and has always been willing to take on extra work, stay late, or work on weekends when needed.

Developmental Needs

■ *Ability to set priorities and juggle two or more jobs at once*: I have found that John tends to get lost in detail on a significant percentage of his jobs. He has difficulty setting priorities and handling more than two assignments at a time without putting in a lot of extra hours to meet his quotas. John agrees that this is a problem.

In the future, he will discuss assignments with me to determine which ones are more important, and we will establish a work priority list for him. I will monitor this procedure, and in three months we'll meet again to decide if this approach solves the problem.

■ *Need for additional training in hydraulic equipment*: John needs to develop his skills in handling the hydraulic equipment we use to mill heavy-machinery parts. He did not have much opportunity on his previous job to use this type of equipment. I have spoken to him about this, and he is willing to attend night classes at the local vocational school.

John continues to be a real asset to our shop. I expect that his performances will improve still further in the coming months.

KB:ifs

POLICY STATEMENT

Policy statements announce a new policy or changes in an established policy, or serve as a reminder to observe a policy. When writing such memos, keep these tips in mind:

■ Make sure your subject line indicates whether the policy is new or revised. Otherwise the readers might skip the memo, thinking they already know what the policy says.

■ If appropriate, state the reasons for the new policy or for revisions or changes in an old one.

■ Give clear instructions for following the policy, but make them sound more like guidelines than restrictions or penalties.

■ Use headings and lists where appropriate to help the readers grasp key points.

(Any organization)

To: All Employees
From: Helen Roark, Director of Human Resources
Date: June 26, 19—
Subject: NEW POLICY: FINDER'S FEE FOR NEW HIRES

Do you know someone who is a perfect match for the jobs available here at Boswell & Craine? Now both you and the person you refer can benefit. The president of Boswell & Craine has authorized me to institute an employee Finder's Fee program. For every job applicant you refer to the company who is hired and remains on the job for six months, you will receive $100 as a finder's fee.

Criteria for job candidates:
To be eligible for the finder's fee, you must make sure that the person you refer meets the following criteria:

- Be 21 years of age or over
- Have at least a high school diploma and be qualified for the particular position he or she is applying for
- Have no prior employment record with Boswell & Craine
- Remain on the job for six months and receive a "satisfactory" or better rating in the first performance appraisal

Procedures for Obtaining Finder's Fee:
Please follow these procedures to ensure that you receive proper credit for your finder's fee.

1. Refer all job candidates to Frieda Getz in Human Resources.

2. If the person or persons you refer are hired, fill out a "Finder's Fee" form and return it to Frieda.

3. If the new hire stays six months and receives a "satisfactory" or better rating, you will be sent the Finder's Fee form again. Sign and date the form, and return it to Frieda. You will receive your check within three to five working days.

Boswell & Craine prides itself on its top quality work force. We feel that no one knows better than you how to find job candidates that measure up to our standards. Our Finder's Fee policy should make it more rewarding for everyone to help the firm hire only the best qualified people. If you have any questions regarding the policy, contact Frieda Getz at ex. 223.

HR:ysh

PROBLEMS, pointing out
Problems are easiest to solve when they are detected early. If you see a problem, point it out as soon as possible, stating clearly what the

problem is and suggesting possible solutions. If appropriate, mention any deadline by which a solution must be found. Tell your readers only what is pertinent to the situation; don't overwhelm them with details or dump the problem in their laps without offering suggestions or options.

(Management consultant firm)

To: Wendell Sims, Vice President
From: Jean O'Mara, Report Production Supervisor
Date: October 3, 19—
Subject: INCREASE IN PRINTING LOAD

Since the firm expanded its consulting services last year, Report Production has experienced a steady increase in its printing load. We now print over 20 reports a week, compared with 10 reports only eight months ago. If this growth rate continues, it will place a severe strain on our current capacity, causing delays in completing client reports and in-house printing jobs. Although we have contracted some of our printing overload to outside print shops, the cost is prohibitive—nearly $4.00 per page versus $1.00 per page for in-house printing. We need to find a more permanent, economical solution to the problem before it gets worse.

I do not know what the budget will allow in this case, but I can suggest at least three possible solutions to this problem.

- Purchase a second printing machine and hire another printer. We can get a good price on rebuilt machines.
- Contract with an outside print shop to take on our overload at a reduced price. We can guarantee them a minimum dollar amount per month.
- Divide the report production work between our office and the New York office. Their production department has twice the capacity of ours.

I would like to discuss this matter with you at your earliest convenience. The problem needs to be solved before this coming January when we receive our heaviest work loads.

JOM:jfb

PROCEDURES

When writing a memo explaining procedures, indicate whether these are new or revised procedures. Begin by providing an overview of what they cover and why the readers should bother to learn them. Give the steps in order and explain each step carefully, giving illustrations or examples where appropriate. Use headings, lists, attachments, or other devices to help the readers to understand the procedures.

(Textbook company)

To: Linda Blaine, Assistant Manager, Regional Sales
From: Jenny Gilbert-Hastings, Manager, Regional Sales
Date: April 9, 19—
Attachments: New Sales Report Formats
Subject: NEW PROCEDURE FOR REPORTING SALES
PERFORMANCE

We are instituting a new procedure for reporting monthly individual sales performances of our staff. Instead of preparing a single list of salespeople and their quotas each month, we will use two separate formats to record monthly sales performance (see attached samples).

The change will make it easier to track individual sales activity and to reward the top sellers in our region. The procedure for reporting total regional sales will remain the same.

To fill out the new forms properly, follow these steps:

1. *Sales performance under quota*: The first report records the names and sales figures of only those salespeople who have sold *less than 90 percent* of the monthly quota. Include the name of the salesperson, her/his territory, what books she/he sells, and all sales figures for the past month. Date and sign the form.

2. *Sales performance above quota*: The second report records the names and sales figures of those salespeople who have sold *more than 110 percent* of their monthly quota. The report should also contain the name, territory, book products, and sales figures of each salesperson. Again, date and sign the form.

3. Turn in the forms along with your report on total regional sales for the month.

This new procedure will go into effect May 1. Our sales force has been doing a superb job, and these reports should help us to recognize their efforts more quickly.

JGH:jkc

PROGRESS REPORT

Progress reports are an excellent means of keeping your colleagues, subordinates, or superiors abreast of events as they unfold. These memos are particularly useful when you have been given an assignment and your boss wants periodic updates on your progress. You have an opportunity to point out problems, commend workers who have given extra efforts or shown unusual resourcefulness, and ask for advice or further instructions.

Summarize project status or progress in the first paragraph, followed by actions, details, and comments on the project so far. Be straightforward about problems but maintain an optimistic rather than a defeatist tone. If you need approval or further information from the reader for the next steps, state what you need and when you need it. Close with a restatement of the reader's expectations for the project and when he or she can expect completion.

(Software firm)

To: Rupert Collingswood, President
From: Wade Turpin, Manager, New Products
Date: May 12, 19—
Subject: PROGRESS ON FILEHOLDER SOFTWARE PROGRAM

Here is a brief rundown on the status of our new FileHolder program. In the past three months our designers have made great progress solving two remaining problems. Specifically:

■ We reconfigured the file and directory operations so that the user can input even fairly complex commands with only a few keystrokes. With the old configuration users had to go back to the menu each time they wanted to view, print, move, rename, or lock up a file. Now they simply type in the file name and a command (PRINT, VIEW, MOVE) and the computer complies.

■ We worked out all the glitches in the backup and restore functions. Previously, only part of the file could be restored. Now the program will restore the entire file.

At the present time, we are working on the last remaining problem: speeding up the selective copying process. As the program now stands, the user selects files to back up and then has to wait for the computer to cycle through the entire file directory.

Our designers feel they can improve the process so that the computer searches only for file names, which would require considerably less computer time. They assure me they will have the entire FileHandler program completed and ready for field testing in two to three weeks. I will assign Lynn Dexter to start work on the users' manual this week. We have enough documentation for her to begin outlining basic functions.

I believe this new product will be everything we envisioned six months ago: a powerful software for handling large files and data bases in business, education, and government. I'll keep you informed of our progress.

WT:cck

PROMOTION

Announcing a promotion can serve not only to point out someone's achievement but to motivate other employees. However, to have the maximum effect the memo should be sent immediately following the promotion or job title change. In your memo, outline briefly the individual's new responsibilities, past accomplishments, and other qualifications that led to the promotion. Your tone should show confidence and pride in the employee's achievement.

(Retail department store)

To: All Employees
From: Gail Sasaki, Store Manager
Date: January 5, 19—
Subject: PROMOTION OF STEVE SYNDER TO SUPERVISOR

It is my pleasure to announce that Steve Synder has been promoted to supervisor of our Customer Service Department, effective January 15, 19—. Steve's first job will be to coordinate a major storewide customer survey to help improve our service.

A graduate of the Calumet Commercial College, Steve started as a floor salesperson in our Men's Wear department. He then transferred to Customer Service to handle our complaint department and to investigate customers' faulty merchandise claims. His excellent work resulted in a 13 percent reduction in customer complaints.

Please join me in congratulating Steve on his new position. We wish him continued success in his fine career.

GS:rgh

PROPOSALS

Proposals can initiate a chain of events that may result in an action as simple as changing suppliers or as dramatic as launching a new business venture. A well-prepared and -presented proposal can give your idea its best chance of success.

- Give the reader the overall scope of the proposal in the first paragraph. If appropriate, include time and cost estimates.
- List the details of your proposal in order of importance. Interpret the details for your readers, telling them what the specific aspects of your proposal mean to them and to the company.
- Use facts, expert opinion, market surveys, or other data that will lend weight and credibility to your ideas.
- Indicate how the proposal might be implemented and which individuals and departments might handle specific tasks.

(Accounting firm)

To: Lorette Hayes, Partner
From: Carla Dickerson, Partner
Date: November 11, 19—
Subject: NEW CONSULTING BUSINESS UNIT

We've always agreed that one of the keys to our success as an accounting firm has been our ability to create new services related to emerging business trends. In this era of mergers and acquisitions, I anticipate a growing need for management advisory and support services on the part of many companies vulnerable to takeover or buyout. Therefore, I propose that we create a special management consulting team whose goal would be to help such companies remain independent.

I think we could create this new business unit quickly, with relatively little start-up cost.

■ *Potential market*: I estimate the market at about 250,000 companies who are in a vulnerable position and would benefit from our services. We have already served as accounting consultants to a number of these firms, giving us a natural introduction into this market.

■ *Consulting team*: We could create the team out of our current staff, shifting Bob Wheeler and Pauline Rush from accounting and Penny Lodge and Pat Sandish from auditing. These four people have the necessary management background and experience to be excellent advisors and consultants to our potential clients.

■ *Services offered*: Our services would focus on the strategic planning level. We could help companies set product and financial goals that would allow them to avoid being taken over, bought out, or squeezed between rivals. We know from experience the major pitfalls vulnerable companies need to avoid and the strategic planning steps they need to take.

If they decide to accept a merger offer, we can help them to negotiate the transaction. Either way, we can provide valuable services enabling companies to make the best deals.

■ *Start-up time and costs*: The team could be assembled in one week, giving us time to reassign current responsibilities and to create the business consulting unit. We would then need to produce press and advertising materials letting people know of our new services. That may take from two to three weeks; add another month for direct mailings and cold calls. We could have the whole unit in operation by March or April. Total cost: I estimate about $75,000.

I realize this new venture is a shift from our traditional business. But it is more of an extension of our current services than a detour in a new direction. I think the volume of our business could at least double if we undertake this venture.

Let me know what you think tomorrow after the morning staff meeting.

CD

PROTESTS

Protests, like complaints, single out an action, attitude, or situation that the writer finds objectionable. If you need to write a protest memo, try to keep your emotions under reasonable control. State your position, but offer solutions, suggestions, or alternatives to change what you find objectionable without violating the other person's rights. You want your protest to produce constructive action, not just an angry reaction.

(Law firm)

To: Jerry Townsend, Esq.
From: Gloria Van Dyne, Esq.
Date: September 30, 19—
Subject: METAL SCULPTURE IN CENTRAL LOBBY

Normally I leave matters of artistic merit to your discretion, but I must protest the placement of the Crowe metal sculpture in the central lobby. The artwork has become something of a hazard. Its long, spiny tendrils catch on clients' trousers, coats, mufflers, and briefcases and are sharp enough to tear cloth.

I would hate for our law firm to find itself on the wrong end of a personal damages suit. Can we move the sculpture into the main conference room or somewhere less hazardous? Please advise.

GVD:prt
cc: Bruce Borland, Associate

REASSURANCE

Whenever someone has failed or is unsure of their position, job, or value, they may need a message of reassurance. You can send them a brief memo expressing your confidence in their abilities and lending words of encouragement. Such a message can be a morale booster and make a discouraged employee try twice as hard the next time around.

In your reassurance memo, mention specific qualities or accomplishments that you feel show the person's true value. If you are reassuring a group, word your memo as if you were speaking to each member individually.

(Police department)

To: All Precinct Officers
From: Tom English, Precinct Commander
Date: February 6, 19—
Subject: INTERNAL INVESTIGATIONS

Whenever any police officers are investigated for misconduct, all of you suffer public mistrust and suspicion. But when you hear rumors that your own department also suspects you, it's enough to make even the most dedicated officer want to quit the force.

I want to reassure each of you that the internal investigations under way are targeted at only a few officers. The misconduct of these men DOES NOT reflect in any way on your own work. Your integrity and loyal service will stand you in good stead throughout the investigations.

You have my full support during this difficult time. I have personally informed Internal Affairs that I intend to be present during all questioning of officers under my command. We have worked together too long not to stand together now.

TE:ghl

cc: Stephen Ford, Police Commissioner
 Tyrone Anhauer, Director of Internal Affairs

RECOMMENDATIONS

Recommendations can be a good word put in for a person, cause, or course of action. In most cases you will be asked for your recommendations by a third party. In writing such memos, state your overall recommendation up front. Follow with specific details that support your stand and close with an offer to discuss the matter further or to supply additional information if the reader wishes to follow up.

(Television station)

To: Jolene Sekowitz, WTRZ Station Manager
From: Terry Laughton, News Director
Date: May 24, 19—
Subject: RECOMMENDATION FOR NEWS DIRECTOR REPLACEMENT

You asked for my recommendations regarding my replacement when I retire in August. I know you favor hiring a news director from outside the station, but I strongly recommend that you consider Carol McMoran for the job.

During the two years Carol has worked as assistant news director, she has proved to be one of the brightest, most professional people I have ever known in the business. Carol is an excellent news editor, producer, and critic. Her suggestions and changes have made Channel 23 one of the leading news stations in the region. She is also highly respected by the staff—and they're not an easy group to please!

Rather than go on in exhaustive detail about Carol's qualifications, I suggest we discuss the matter personally. I'd be happy to meet with you at your earliest convenience.

TL:edr

REFERENCES

At some point in your career you will be called on to provide a reference for a subordinate, friend, or colleague. The individual may be seeking a job outside your firm or may be transferring within the firm. Keep the following guidelines in mind when you write your reference memo:

■ If you are writing for a subordinate, describe the person's major responsibilities and dates under your supervision. If for a friend or colleague, mention how long you have known the person and in what capacity.

■ Briefly describe both strengths and weaknesses and any personal characteristics that make the individual a good candidate for the job. Be specific (*not* "he has a good personality," *but* "he is well liked by his co-workers and often moderates disputes").

■ If your relationship with your employee has not been smooth, don't let personal feelings affect your evaluation. Give the person the benefit of the doubt—perhaps the difficulty between you was the result of a personality clash. Another supervisor might get along with the person better.

(Hotel chain)

To: Margaret Hutton, Manager, Regency Hotel I
From: Lawrence Paine, Manager, Regency Hotel II
Date: August 20, 19—
Subject: REFERENCE: PAUL COSTELLO

I am happy to see Paul Costello start up the career ladder with his transfer to your organization. But I must admit that I find it hard to let him go. Paul has worked with me as an assistant manager trainee for two years; and I have never supervised a more dedicated, energetic, and intelligent employee.

Paul was responsible for overseeing all housewares and cleaning staff, negotiating contracts with tradespeople, and supervising grounds work. Many times in his two-year stay, he accepted responsibilities far beyond those normally assigned to someone in his position. In one instance, he had to take over the restaurant manager's job for a week and handled the work with efficiency and excellent judgment. He has a great flair for working with all levels of people from the cleaning maids to the vice president in charge of operations.

If Paul has any faults at all, they tend to be on the side of demanding too much of himself. If you give him an assignment to have the floors polished, for example, you may find him with polisher in hand, helping the maintenance people. You may want to supervise him closely for the first few weeks, from a discreet distance, of course, to make sure he is not being overzealous.

I believe his ability to assume additional responsibilities is the surest sign that he is ready to step into his own full-time position as your assistant manager. You will be getting an exceptional employee, and he will be getting a well-deserved promotion. I wish you both the best.

LP:hgf

REFUSALS/REGRETS

Because you can't accept every invitation, it's good to know how to write a refusal or regrets memo. In some cases, turning down an invitation may be sensitive, such as refusing a superior or a group you don't want to offend. Use the diamond sequence in such cases, softening the blow by first recognizing the honor of being invited.

(Any company, colleague to colleague)

To: Ted Ingram
From: Diane Lafferty

Date: November 13, 19—
Subject: AWARDS DINNER

Thanks so much for your personal note inviting me and my husband to the awards dinner being held in your honor. Unfortunately, my family and I will be in Europe during that week and will be unable to attend the dinner.

You richly deserve the "Retailer of the Year" award. I think you're one of the best in the business. Please accept my warmest congratulations on earning this award. I only wish I could be there when you receive it.

DL

(Subordinate to superior)

To: Mark Halman, Vice President of Sales
From: Sara Strickland, Manager
Date: March 3, 19—
Subject: APRIL COMPANY SALES RALLY

I was honored to receive your invitation to speak at next month's company sales rally. The rallies always meant a great deal to me as a fledgling salesperson, and I still enjoy them.

Unfortunately, being a manager means I am still on the road a great deal. Much as I would have enjoyed discussing successful sales techniques at the rally, I regret I must decline your invitation. I will be out of town that week negotiating the Rivers contract in Philadelphia.

Please keep me in mind for future rallies. Perhaps I can serve as speaker for the May or June event. Once again, thank you for your invitation.

SS:ret

REMINDERS

A reminder can be a general announcement to the entire firm or a gentle prod to jog an individual's memory. Put the word *reminder* in the subject line or first sentence to alert your readers; state in the first paragraph what you wish to remind them about. In the body of the memo, repeat the original information in your first message — time, date, place, event, purpose, deadlines, and so on. If you are sending the reminder because of a change in previous arrangements, highlight the change.

(Travel agency)

To: All Employees
From: Veronica Presnell, Office Manager
Date: June 28, 19 —
Subject: RECARPETING AGENCY OFFICE

Just a reminder that we will be laying new carpeting in the entire office over this weekend. When you leave work on Friday, please make sure all boxes, wastebaskets, chairs, and other lightweight items are moved out into the hallway.

Also, please clear off your desk tops. You may either put your belongings in your desk drawers (which should be locked) or pack them in boxes. Label your boxes to help you find your belongings easily on Monday morning. Thank you.

VP:ghs

REPLY/REJOINDER. See also INQUIRY, REQUESTS.
One of the most frequent questions memo senders ask of their readers is "Did you get the memo I sent you on...?" When people make an inquiry or request, or when they lodge a complaint or protest, they expect some response from the readers. As a result, the reply/rejoinder is an essential part of the communication process in a company.

A good rule of thumb is to send off a reply within a day of receiving a memo, particularly if you know you will be delayed in giving a more complete answer. Even a brief note simply letting the sender know you received the memo and are considering it reassures the person that the communication process between the two of you is alive and well.

(Scrap processing plant)

To: Albert Gutenberg, Shop Foreman
From: Dick Conners, Plant Manager
Date: August 5, 19—
Subject: <u>Faulty Ventilation in Scrap Processing Area</u>

Al, I got your memo describing the ventilation problem in your shop area. If it's as bad as you say, I agree you and your men shouldn't be expected to work in such a hazardous environment. I've got Bob Johnson in Building Repair and Maintenance working on this problem right now. Until the ventilation is repaired, reassign your workers to the shipping dock. Let's hope we can fix this problem fast.

DC:jsw

REPORTS, general
One of the most common uses of the memo report is to summarize information gained at seminars, conferences, meetings, or conventions. A memo report can range from two to twenty pages or more. Regardless of length, the organizing principles are the same:

■ Summary of the topic and/or recommendations
■ An item-by-item discussion of each topic covered using headings and lists to help the reader through your report
■ Closing paragraphs that recap the major findings or recommendations

(Small company producing beer, one partner to another)

To: Peter Nettleson
From: Kelly Johannsen
Date: August 2, 19—
Subject: SEMINAR ON SMALL BUSINESS DEVELOPMENT

Last week I attended the day-long seminar on small business development put on by the Small Business Administration. It opened my eyes to a number of new opportunities to help us develop and market our product. I thought I'd share a few key points that could be the most beneficial to our company.

SMALL BUSINESS NEWSLETTER
The Department of Commerce and Community Affairs Small Business Assistance Bureau (in cooperation with the federal Small Business Administration) now publishes a quarterly newsletter for the state's small businesses. The newsletter offers a wealth of information about state and federal assistance programs, legislative updates, capital markets, marketing and distribution, and state and local small business agencies. I recommend we subscribe to the newsletter; cost is about $120 per year.

STATE UNIVERSITY TECHNOLOGY CENTER
The state university has opened a technology transfer center to aid small businesses. The center has access to industry, academic, and government resources. They can help us determine how the latest technological advances can be applied to our business. The center offers advice, fundings, and even custom-designed technological applications. Bernie Culpepper is the contact at the center.

ADVERTISING AND INSURANCE
Advertising received a lot of attention at the seminar. We've been juggling various ad ideas for a while, but the seminar gave us a step-by-step formula to follow before making a final decision.

- Decide on your target market.
- Decide on a budget, even if it's a rough estimate.

■ Talk to salespeople from various media. Ask them to help you estimate advertising costs.

■ Ask other local business people about their experiences with advertising.

■ Determine which is the best ad medium for you.

The speakers also suggested hiring an advertising consultant or agency, especially if we are considering television or radio commercials. They reminded us that small businesses shouldn't overlook cable television advertising — a possibility we haven't really considered.

Part of the afternoon session was devoted to the importance and pitfalls of insuring your small business. I won't go into details here, but this is an area we definitely have to study. Many property and casualty insurance companies now offer policies especially designed for small businesses.

CONCLUSION

As you can see, the seminar was well worth the time and money we spent. I think we should start taking advantage of some of the opportunities out there and start making those hard decisions we've been avoiding. Let's set aside time next week to talk about this. Our company needs to be on much better footing for the next decade.

KJ:wef

REQUESTS

When you are asking for information, follow these guidelines:

■ Tell the reader in the first paragraph what information you need and why.

■ List your questions in order of priority. If the recipient can't answer all your questions, at least have her/him answer the most important ones.

■ Provide any information the reader may need to prepare a reply — measurements, dimensions, figures, color requirements, and so on. The more background work you do and the less the reader has to do, the faster you'll get a reply.

■ Emphasize when you need the information. Even if there is no immediate hurry, you are likely to get quicker results if you give the recipient a firm due date.

■ If appropriate, provide incentive for readers to cooperate. Tell them "what's in it for them."

If you are responding to a request, make sure you state your information clearly and in a convenient format. Use bulleted or numbered lists, headings, or other devices to help the reader grasp the details and understand what you have to say. Keep the request close at hand to be sure you have answered all of the sender's questions.

(Any company)

To: All Department Managers
From: Elaine Cranshaw, Budget Director
Date: April 5, 19—
Attachment: Budget Estimate Form and instructions
Subject: Requests for Budget Estimates

It's that time of year for taxes and budget preparation—everyone's favorite activities. This year, however, it should be easier to formulate your budget estimates than to do your taxes.

We have developed a new form, complete with instructions (see attached), to help you estimate your budgetary needs and justify all departmental expenses. Please make a note of the following due dates for preparing and submitting your information:

	Initial review	Revised budget due	Final approval
Operations	5/1	5/12	5/27
Production	5/2	5/13	5/29
Personnel	5/3	5/14	5/31
Marketing	5/4	5/15	6/2
Distribution	5/5	5/16	6/4

These dates should provide ample time to evaluate your budgetary needs and give us time to consolidate the overall budget by the June 15 deadline. If you cannot meet your deadlines, contact me *immediately* to arrange alternate due dates.

Please provide specific justification for all requested budget categories. If you need information on tuition and related expenses for educational and professional development courses, contact Bruce Hopland, Director of Training.

With careful organization and planning, we can meet our budget deadlines with time to spare. We might even get our tax returns filed on time.

EC:hjd

RESIGNATIONS
Messages dealing with resignations have a single point: an individual is leaving the organization. Such memos can range from cold, matter-of-fact messages to an expression of one's gratitude and fond memories.

Even if you are leaving under difficult or strained circumstances, it's best to keep your tone neutral. Nothing lasting can be gained by firing off a parting shot before you walk out the door. Parting shots have an unsettling way of boomeranging.

(Office of National Labor Relations Board)

To: All Employees
From: Carlos Fuentes
Date: March 6, 19—
Subject: MY RESIGNATION

As some of you may already know, I am resigning my position here at the NLRB on June 1 to pursue a career in the private sector. I have accepted a position as senior consultant with the legal firm Hyatt, Ortiz,

& Granadas. I am leaving with a mixture of excitement and regret, because I have greatly enjoyed working with all of you. You've been not just colleagues but my friends as well.

My work here over the past 11 years has been deeply fulfilling. It has been a pleasure to be associated with one of the most respected offices in the federal government. Together we've accomplished a great deal, and we have much to be proud of.

I sincerely hope that our friendship will not end with my departure. My best wishes for you all in the coming years.

CF:tr

RUMORS, handling

Every company has its own rumor mill. Most of the time rumors fly harmlessly, but in some instances you will need to ground them with the truth. State the rumor and the correction in the first paragraph, substituting "concern" or some other more neutral word for "rumor." Acknowledge the kernel of truth in the rumor, which will add credibility to your message. Do not point the finger at the rumor mongers unless it is absolutely necessary—no one likes to be labeled a gossiper. End on a positive, casual note.

(A large department store)

To: All Employees
From: Jim Schaefer, Chairman and CEO
Subject: JACK KELSON'S DEPARTURE

It has come to my attention that the departure of Vice President of Operations Jack Kelson has caused some anxiety among the store's employees that Casey's may soon be sold. Although Jack's departure was unexpected, we have no plans to sell the store.

As we all know, Jack is a particularly skilled and experienced executive. Over the years, he has received many tempting offers from various companies. He finally received one he couldn't refuse—an offer to form his own consulting company — and he decided to leave Casey's within the month.

We are currently conducting a search for his replacement. It is a tribute to his ability that his sudden departure could cause such a stir among all the employees. We wish him all the best in his new venture.

JS:rr

SAFETY PRECAUTIONS

Safety in the workplace should be a major concern of all employees in a company, but the managers set the tone. Whenever a potential safety problem is brought to your attention, write a memo immediately pointing out the problem and how to correct it.

If the reason for the safety practice is not obvious, explain to your readers why it is company policy. You want to elicit their cooperation, but remind them of the consequences if they fail to observe the practice.

(Plastics injection-molding factory)

To: All Employees
From: Sam Browne, Factory Supervisor
Date: January 19, 19 —
Subject: SAFETY PRECAUTION-NONSLIP BOOTS

A number of workers are not wearing their nonslip safety boots while working in the clean room. Please wear these boots AT ALL TIMES when you are working in the clean-room area.

We issued the boots last May after a series of accidents in which workers slipped on the clean-room floor. In one case, an employee struck his head on the floor and had to have 15 stitches in his scalp.

For your own protection, make it a habit to put on the boots before you enter the clean room. Let's make our factory a safe place to work. Thank you for your cooperation.

SB:uf

SEASONAL GREETINGS

At various times of the year, a seasonal greetings memo to employees adds a personal touch to your business environment. Besides wishing employees a happy holiday season, you can highlight accomplishments of the past year or past few months. Be brief but personal, adding your own sincere wishes.

(Any organization)

To: All Bank Tellers

From: Susanne Gale, Manager

Date: December 28, 19—

Subject: BEST WISHES FOR THE NEW YEAR

I want to take this opportunity to wish each of you a happy and prosperous New Year. You are part of an outstanding group, and your friendliness and professionalism keep our customers coming back. I look forward to another year of working together. Happy holidays to each one of you!

SG:opk

SELF-PROTECTION

This message is also known as a CYA (cover your anatomy) memo. It's purpose is strictly political: to create a record of your action, point of view, situation, or feelings about a given issue. In the light of subsequent developments, the memo is on hand to protect you against misunderstandings or blame. You may want to send copies to everyone involved in the situation.

(Academic library)

To: Wayne Holder, Head Librarian

From: Ruth Downing, EDP Manager

Date: November 8, 19—

Subject: COMPUTERIZED INVENTORY SYSTEM

I am currently moving ahead with preparations to implement the library's new computerized card catalog inventory system. As you requested, I will not arrange to integrate the new system with our other, more extensive data bases.

In my opinion, however, it is a mistake not to integrate our system with these data bases. Our school is growing, and more students will want to access professional journals held in other libraries. It may be that we can find another, more economical way to network. We can only wait and see.

RD:dfh
cc: Grace Fielding, Chancellor

SOLICITATIONS

When you solicit for contributions or volunteers, keep your tone light and informal. Use an upbeat opening to get the readers' attention, then state your request for participation. Tell your readers exactly what you want them to do and how to do it: make it easy for them to participate. If appropriate, tell them how their contribution or volunteer efforts will benefit them. Finally, mention others who support your cause, but let your own enthusiasm be your best persuader.

(Any organization)

To: All Employees
From: Orleen L. Whyte, President
Date: November 5, 19—
Subject: CONTRIBUTIONS TO UNITED WAY FUND

This year we'd like your help in setting a record goal for our company's contribution to United Way. We'd like to increase our share from $55,000 to $60,000—an all-time high. As our current sales figures show, nothing is beyond this group once they set their minds on a goal!

Whether you pledge 1 percent, 2 percent, or 5 percent of your salary, consider giving just a little more than last year. The United Way sponsors many worthwhile community programs, such as medical care for children, help for the homeless, and care for the elderly. This year you can even specify which program you would like your funds to support (see attached brochure).

If you pledge 5 percent or more of your salary, the company will match your contribution dollar for dollar. This will double the value of your pledge to United Way.

This Thursday someone from your department will distribute pledge cards. Whether or not you decide to make a contribution, please fill out the card and return it to Personnel. I urge each of you to consider giving some amount, no matter how small. You can help the company meet its goal and give hope to a lot of people who need your help. Thank you.

OLW:kwt

Attachment: United Way brochure

SUGGESTIONS. See IDEAS.

SYMPATHY. See CONDOLENCES.

TRANSMITTAL. See also COVERING MEMO.
Transmittal memos, like covering memos, accompany a document sent to an individual or group. Unlike a covering memo, however, the transmittal message is meant to serve as a summary of the document's contents and not simply as a message saying, "Here is your report." Use the following guidelines for writing your transmittal memos:

■ In the first paragraph, mention the document you are transmitting, whether further information is to follow, and the reason the document is being sent.
■ Give a brief summary of the significant findings, recommendations, or information contained in the document.
■ Anticipate and answer questions readers may have about any unusual data (e.g., survey results are contrary to expectations).

■ Give a brief interpretation of the data. (Are the survey results reliable? What do they mean?)
■ Let readers know how they can obtain further information or copies of original research material.

(Computer software company)

To: Dorthea Wexler, President and CEO
From: Wesley Anderson, Director of Human Resources
Date: July 9, 19—
Attachment: Report on Survey Results
Subject: EMPLOYEE EXIT INTERVIEW SURVEY

Attached please find the completed report summarizing our results of the exit interview survey we conducted. As you requested, we interviewed all employees who left the company within the past 12 months and asked them to fill out a survey on their reasons for leaving. The results seem to justify your concern about our lack of adequate employee training programs.

Survey Results:
A quick glance at the survey results shows that career and human relations concerns outweighed monetary issues for over 90 percent of the employees surveyed. The principal reasons for leaving are listed in order of frequency and importance.

■ Limited opportunities for advancement in the company (56 out of 62 respondents; rating 9.0 on a scale of 10)
■ Boredom with their jobs (53 out of 62 respondents; rating 8.2)
■ Dissatisfaction with management (48 out of 62 respondents; rating 7.3)
■ Inadequate salaries or benefits (35 out of 62 respondents; rating 4.5)
■ Lack of recognition for work done (34 out of 62 respondents; rating 4.2)

I am confident about the accuracy of the results. We cross-correlated all answers and found them to be 92 percent reliable. To encourage employees to be honest, I assured them their responses would remain anonymous.

Interpretation of Results:

The survey clearly shows that the respondents place high value on career development and personal satisfaction with their work, what Maslow would call "self-actualization needs." Because these employees are fairly representative of our work force, I believe we can assume that our current employees share the same concerns.

In my opinion we should proceed with our plans to develop a series of job enrichment programs for employees. I believe we can draw on our management staff for instructors — several of our managers have taught professional classes before. We can discuss the details in next week's staff meeting.

If you would like to look at the original surveys, let me know. I have all the files in my office. I believe this project has given us the proof we need to go ahead with our developmental programs.

WA:rty

VIEWING WITH ALARM. See also ACTION, call for; PROTESTS.
This message is like sounding a red alert to catch someone's attention, whether that of a subordinate or a superior. It can be used to voice your concern about someone's deteriorating performance or to point out a situation that is getting out of hand.

When you write this message, be sure to stick to the facts. Avoid the two pitfalls of crying wolf or exaggerating the condition simply to attract attention. Tell the reader what is going on, why it is hazardous or self-defeating, and what the consequences might be. Be specific about what you want the reader to do.

(Machine-parts manufacturing firm)

To: Ben Wayne, Vice President, Operations
From: Mark Olson, Quality Control Inspector
Date: September 12, 19—
Subject: FAULTY PERFORMANCE OF ASSEMBLY LINE PERSONNEL

Although some may say it's my job to be picky, there are times when I feel compelled to speak out and this is one of them. Over the past month I've noticed an alarming decline of quality on the #45 parts assembly line. These parts are inserted in the motors of earth-moving machinery. If they malfunction, they can cause serious accidents, with possible loss of life.

Workers on the #45 line are not assembling the parts correctly. They leave off washers, fail to tighten nuts adequately, allow dirt and other particles to get into the bearings, and even damage the outer casings, making it difficult to obtain a proper fit with engine parts. I have spoken to the assembly line foreman about this problem, but so far he has taken no action.

I'm sure you'll agree that this problem requires immediate attention. If an accident that is traced to our faulty parts does occur, the company could be faced with a multimillion-dollar lawsuit. I would appreciate your looking into this matter.

MO:sde

WELCOME. See ORIENTATION/WELCOME.

COMMONLY CONFUSED WORDS

▼

The meaning and spelling of the following words are often confused. Practice using them until the correct usage is second nature to you.

accept, except

> *accept* — (verb) to take, agree
> We *accept* the offer.
> *except* — (adverb) excluding, omitting
> Order everything *except* the printer ribbons.

advice, advise

> *advice* — (noun) opinion, counsel
> I need a lawyer's *advice*.
> *advise* — (verb) to counsel
> The court *advised* him of his rights.

affect, effect

> *affect* — (verb) to influence, change
> The price changes *affect* the entire industry.
> *effect* — (noun) impression, results; (verb) to cause
> The legislation had a profound *effect* on foreign trade.
> It has *effected* a complete change in tariffs.

already, all ready

already — (adverb) even now
They *already* made a bid for our company.
all ready — (adjective) all prepared
They are *all ready* to make the trip.

assent, ascent

assent — (verb) to agree; (noun) permission
He *assented* to your request.
You need the manager's *assent* to proceed.
ascent — (noun) advancement
She made her final *ascent* to the mountain's summit this morning.

capital, capitol

capital — (noun) wealth; seat of government
We're short of *capital* this quarter.
This week I'm traveling to the nation's *capital*.
capitol — (noun) government building
They voted to refurbish the *capitol* over the next year.

cite, site, sight

cite — (verb) refer to, state; to serve notice on
The prosecutor *cited* his reasons for dropping all charges.
Our chemical plant has been *cited* for EPA violations.
site — (noun) location
Have they chosen a *site* for the new insurance building?
sight — (noun) scene
The stock exchange was quite a *sight* on "Black Monday."

cloths, clothes

cloths — (noun) pieces of cloth
Use *cloths* to polish the finished die-cut pieces.
clothes — (noun) wearing apparel
Her *clothes* make a very odd fashion statement.

complement, compliment

complement — (noun) something that completes
A chocolate mousse is the perfect *complement* to the meal.
compliment — (verb) to say something good about someone; (noun) a
flattering remark
The boss *complimented* Jean on her work. His *compliment* made her
feel all her efforts had been worth it.

consul, council, counsel

consul — (noun) foreign embassy official
We need to talk to the *consul* from Taiwan about our trade idea.
council — (noun) official body
Carl won election to the city *council* after a bitter fight.
counsel — (verb) to advise; (noun) legal advisor
You should have expert *counsel* regarding your claim. Perhaps the
company lawyer will act as your *counsel* in the matter.

dissent, descent, descend

dissent — (noun) disagreement
He cast the only vote in *dissent* of the merger.
descent — (noun) a decline, fall
After a brilliant start, the company experienced a steep *descent* into
bankruptcy.
descend — (verb) to come down
We had to *descend* into the sub-basement to reach the vault.

fewer, less

fewer — (adjective) lower in number (used for individual units,
numbers)
We have five *fewer* workers in our factory than last year.
Let's make *fewer* long distance calls this month.
less — (adjective) reduced amount (used for quantities)
Give us *less* talk and more money.
We have *less* capital to work with on this project.

formerly, formally

> *formerly* — (adverb) previously
> He was *formerly* the president of Safeway.
> *formally* — (adverb) officially
> The President is *formally* sworn into office in January.

imply, infer

> *imply* — (verb) to suggest
> She *implied* that Paul had changed the figures in his report.
> *infer* — (verb) to deduce from evidence
> We found the true figures in the wastebasket; therefore, we can *infer* that Paul did change his report.

it's, its

> *it's* — contraction of *it is* or *it has*
> *It's* (it has) been a tough contract to negotiate.
> After three days of bargaining, I'm glad *it's* (it is) over.
> *its* — possessive form of the pronoun *it*
> The problem is in the computer's hardware, not *its* software.

later, latter

> *later* — (adverb) after a time
> Let's go over this memo *later* today.
> *latter* — (adjective) the last mentioned of two items
> You can fly to New York or Palm Springs. I'll take the *latter*.

lay, lie

> *lie* — (verb) to rest or recline (lie, lay, lain)
> Ned always *lies* down on the job just when you need him. He *lay* around for hours yesterday. I wish he had *lain* in the hallway when the foreman walked by.
> *lay* — (verb) to put or place something (lay, laid, laid)
> I saw Julie *lay* the file down over there. She *laid* it on top of the file cabinet. She has *laid* it there many times before.

lead, led, lead

lead—(verb) to go before, to conduct; (adjective) first
I was asked to *lead* the meeting yesterday.
The *lead* speaker forgot her slides.
led—(past tense of lead) directed.
I *led* the meeting yesterday.
lead—(noun) heavy metal; graphite
We need a *lead* shield to protect us from radiation.

lose, loose, loss

lose—(verb) to misplace
Don't *lose* the report.
loose—(adjective) not fastened down; (adverb) release
The wire is *loose* on this telephone.
Turn Ross *loose* on this project.
loss—(noun) deprivation
Company earnings showed a *loss* for the fourth quarter.

past, passed

past—(adjective) preceding
She's the *past* president of the Associated Press.
passed—(verb form) went by; gone by
She *passed* us on the road.

personal, personnel

personal—(adjective) individual, private
I have *personal* reasons for turning down the job.
personnel—(noun) a department or division; workers
The *personnel* department is now called "human resources."
They keep records on all company *personnel*.

precede, proceed

precede—(verb) to come before
The old policy *precedes* the new one by about four years.
proceed—(verb) to go ahead, to initiate
We can *proceed* with the meeting as soon as everyone arrives.

principle, principal

principle — (noun) rule, standard

One *principle* of good management is knowing when to delegate authority.

principal — (adjective) main, foremost; (noun) superintendent

She's the *principal* reason her agency is on top.

Even her high school *principal* predicted she'd be a success.

quiet, quite

quiet — (adjective) silent

The office is *quiet* at night.

quite — (adverb) completely; to a considerable degree

I *quite* agree that the judge's decision was unfair. The prosecutor also was *quite* upset at the decision.

rise, raise

rise — (verb) to go up, to get up; (noun) reaction

The sun *rises* earlier each morning.

That report certainly got a *rise* out of the president.

raise — (verb) to lift, to bring up; (noun) an increase

Raise the camera higher. If we get this shot just right, we can ask for a *raise*.

sit, set

sit — (verb) to rest or recline.

Arnold had to *sit* on the plane for six hours.

set — (verb) to put or place something

Set the coffee on my desk.

I have to *set* these files in order.

stationary, stationery

stationary — (adjective) still, fixed

I got a new *stationary* monitor.

stationery — (noun) letter paper

Make sure you write that letter on company *stationery*.

than, then

than — (conjunction) after a comparison; when

Our bid is lower *than* theirs. I had no sooner mailed the proposal *than* the new figures arrived.

then — (adverb) next, in that case; (noun) that time

She dialed in the code *then* replaced the receiver.

If you want to make the trip, *then* you'd better leave at six.

By *then*, the last train leaves for the airport.

that, which

that — (conjunction) used to introduce a clause that expresses a supposed or actual fact, a purpose, a result, or a cause. The information added is usually essential to the meaning of the sentence.

Warren told us *that* Carla isn't getting a promotion.

The statement showed *that* our sales were higher this year.

This is the new software *that* doesn't have any manual. (The clause *doesn't have any manual* tells which software among many it is.)

which — (pronoun) used to refer to a specific noun or pronoun in a sentence; often the information introduced is not essential to the meaning of the sentence.

This is the new software, *which* hasn't any manual. (The clause *which hasn't any manual* is simply added information about the new software.)

there, their, they're

there — (adverb) a place

Put the book over *there* by the recorder.

their — possessive form of *they*

Their presentation was a tremendous success.

they're — contraction of *they are*

They're the best presenters in the company.

weather, whether

weather — (noun) climate

Our flight was canceled because of bad *weather*.

whether — (adverb) if; regardless

Do you know *whether* the stock market has gone up? You should sell that stock *whether* you feel like it or not.

who's, whose

who's — contraction of *who is* or *who has*

Who's (who is) setting the agenda for our meeting?

Do you know *who's* (who has) turned in their timesheets?

whose — possessive form of *who*

Whose unmarked floppy disk is this?

you're, your

you're — contraction of *you are*

Andy told me *you're* nervous about using the fax machine.

your — possessive form of *you*

I hate to tell you but *your* document is stuck in the fax.

FREQUENTLY MISSPELLED WORDS

A
abbreviate
absence
abundant
accessible
accommodate
accompanies
accompaniment
accumulate
accuracy
acknowledgment
acquaintance
adequately
admission
admittance
adolescent
advantageous
allege
alliance
analysis
analyze
anonymous

apologetically
apparatus
apparent
appreciate
appropriate
argument
arrangement
arrears
ascertain
association
attendance
authorize
auxiliary
awfully

B
ballet
bankruptcy
beneficial
bibliography
bookkeeper

boulevard
brochure
buffet
bulletin

C
calculation
calendar
camouflage
canceled
cancellation
catalog
catastrophe
category
cellar
cemetery
changeable
choose
chose
colossal
column
commitment

committed
committee
comparative
competent
competition
competitor
complexion
comptroller
conceivable
concise
conscience
conscientious
consciousness
consensus
consistency
contingency
controlling
controversy
correspondence
correspondent
criticize
curriculum

D
debacle
debt
debtor
decadent
deceit
deceive
deference
deferred
dependent
depreciation
description
desirable
detrimental
dilemma
diligence
disastrous
disciple
discrimination
dissatisfaction
division
divisive

E
economical
ecstasy
effect
efficiency
embarrassment
emphasize
endeavor
enforceable
enormous
enthusiastically
entrance
espionage
exaggerate
exaggeration
excel
exceptionally
exhaustion
exhibition
exhibitor
exhilaration
existence
exorbitant
expensive
extension
exuberant

F
facilitate
facilitator
familiar
familiarity
familiarize
fascination
feasible
feminine
financier
foreign
franchise
fraud
fraudulent
freight
fulfill

G
gauge
grammar
grievance
guarantee
guaranty
guidance

H
harassment
hereditary
hindrance
horizontal
hygiene
hypocrisy
hypothetical

I
ideally
idiomatic
illegible
immediately
imperative
implement
incidentally
inconvenience
indemnity
independent
indispensable
inevitable
inflationary
influence
influential
ingenious
initial
initiative
innocent
inoculate
institution
intellectual
interfere
interference
interpretation
interrupt
invoice
irrelevant
irresistible
itemize
itinerary

J
jeopardize
jeopardy
judgment

K
kerosene
knowledge
knowledgeable

L
labeled
laborious
legitimate
leisurely
liable
liability

license
likelihood
livelihood
liquor
livable
loose
lucrative
luxurious

M

magistrate
magnificence
magnificent
maintain
maintenance
majestic
malicious
manageable
mandatory
maneuver
marketable
materialism
measurable
mediator
mediocre
melancholy
metaphor
miniature
miscellaneous
mischievous
misspell
misstatement
mortgage
mosquito

municipal
mysterious

N

naive
naiveté
necessary
necessity
negligible
negotiable
negotiate
neurotic
neutral
ninety
ninth
noticeable

O

objectionable
observant
occasionally
occupant
occurred
occurrence
omission
omitting
opinionated
option
outrageous
overrated

P

pageant
pamphlet

parallel
paralysis
parity
parliament
particularly
pastime
pedestal
penicillin
permanent
permissible
permitted
persistent
personal
personnel
perspiration
phenomenon
physician
picnicking
plausible
politician
possession
practically
precede
precise
preference
preferred
prejudice
presence
prestige
presumption
prevalent
privilege
procedure
proceed

propaganda
prophesy
prove
psychology
pursuant
pursue

Q

qualitative
quality
quantify
quantitative
quantity
questionnaire
quietly
quit
quite

R

rebellion
rebellious
receipt
receive
recommend
recommendation
reconcile
reconciliation
recur
recurrence
reducible
reference
referred
rehearsal
reimburse

reimbursement
relief
relieve
reminiscent
remit
remittance
remitted
repetition
representative
resource
respectfully
responsibility
returnable
reveal
revelation
revenue
routine

S
salable
schedule
scientific
scrutinize
scrutiny
separation
sergeant
serviceable
siege
significant
similar
souvenir
specifically
specimen
sponsor

statistics
strategic
stubbornness
substantial
succeed
succession
superficial
superfluous
superintendent
supersede
supervisor
suppress
surroundings
susceptible
symbolic
symmetrical
synonymous

T
tariff
technical
technician
technology
temperature
tendency
theoretical
tolerance
tolerant
tomorrow
traffic
trafficking
tragedy
tragic
transcend

transmit
transmittal
transparent
tried
twelfth
tyranny

U
unanimous
undoubtedly
uniform
universal
unknown
unmistakable
unnatural
unnecessary
unscrupulous

V
vaccine
vaccination
vacuum
variation
variety
vehicle
vengeance
ventilation
versatile
vigilance
villain
vinegar
volume

W
waive
waiver

warrantee
warranty
whisper
whistle
whole
wholly
withhold

Y
yacht
yawn
yield
young
youth

Z
zealot
zealous
zenith

INDEX